Repair with Self-Care

Repair with Self-Care

Your Guide to the Mom's Hierarchy of Needs

Leslie Forde

JB JOSSEY-BASS
A Wiley Brand

Copyright © 2025 by Leslie Forde. All rights reserved.

Published by John Wiley & Sons, Inc., Hoboken, New Jersey.
Published simultaneously in Canada.

ISBNs: 9781394320158 (Hardback), 9781394320172 (ePDF), 9781394320165 (epub).

No part of this publication may be reproduced, stored in a retrieval system, or transmitted in any form or by any means, electronic, mechanical, photocopying, recording, scanning, or otherwise, except as permitted under Section 107 or 108 of the 1976 United States Copyright Act, without either the prior written permission of the Publisher, or authorization through payment of the appropriate per-copy fee to the Copyright Clearance Center, Inc., 222 Rosewood Drive, Danvers, MA 01923, (978) 750-8400, fax (978) 750-4470, or on the web at www.copyright.com. Requests to the Publisher for permission should be addressed to the Permissions Department, John Wiley & Sons, Inc., 111 River Street, Hoboken, NJ 07030, (201) 748-6011, fax (201) 748-6008, or online at http://www.wiley.com/go/permission.

The manufacturer's authorized representative according to the EU General Product Safety Regulation is Wiley-VCH GmbH, Boschstr. 12, 69469 Weinheim, Germany, e-mail: Product_Safety@wiley.com.

Trademarks: Wiley and the Wiley logo are trademarks or registered trademarks of John Wiley & Sons, Inc. and/or its affiliates in the United States and other countries and may not be used without written permission. Mom's Hierarchy of Needs and TimeCheck are registered trademarks of Mom's Hierarchy of Needs, LLC All other trademarks are the property of their respective owners. John Wiley & Sons, Inc. is not associated with any product or vendor mentioned in this book.

Limit of Liability/Disclaimer of Warranty: While the publisher and author have used their best efforts in preparing this book, they make no representations or warranties with respect to the accuracy or completeness of the contents of this book and specifically disclaim any implied warranties of merchantability or fitness for a particular purpose. No warranty may be created or extended by sales representatives or written sales materials. The advice and strategies contained herein may not be suitable for your situation. You should consult with a professional where appropriate. Further, readers should be aware that websites listed in this work may have changed or disappeared between when this work was written and when it is read. Neither the publisher nor authors shall be liable for any loss of profit or any other commercial damages, including but not limited to special, incidental, consequential, or other damages.

For general information on our other products and services or for technical support, please contact our Customer Care Department within the United States at (800) 762-2974, outside the United States at (317) 572-3993 or fax (317) 572-4002.

Wiley also publishes its books in a variety of electronic formats. Some content that appears in print may not be available in electronic formats. For more information about Wiley products, visit our web site at www.wiley.com.

Library of Congress Control Number: 2025026032 (Print)

Cover Design: Wiley
Cover Image: © stellalevi/Getty Images
Author Photo: © Keith Gabryelski

SKY10122099_071725

Contents

Introduction   vii

Section One: Free Your Mind   1

Chapter 1: Escape from the Tunnel   3
Chapter 2: See the Three Ghosts for What They Are   21
Chapter 3: Emerge from the (Mental) Fog   45

Section Two: Ease Your Workload   57

Chapter 4: Shift, Trim, Eliminate, and Repeat   59
Chapter 5: Overcome Common Boundary Traps   69
Chapter 6: Get Strategic with Your Childcare Support   95
Chapter 7: Outsource or Spouse Source   119

Section Three: Fuel Your Future   141

Chapter 8: Why Health Span Matters to Your Potential   143
Chapter 9: The Importance of Emotional Health   157
Chapter 10: The Magic of Movement   175
Chapter 11: Manage Energy Inputs Including Your Nutrition and Hormonal Health   189
Chapter 12: Make the Space for Learning and Growth   207
Chapter 13: Healthy Adult Relationships and Energetic Space   225

Afterword: Tools You Can Use   239
Acknowledgments   241
Index   245

Introduction

In this book, I have one job: to help you invest more of your time in self-care. That includes everything you need for your well-being and growth, like sleep, movement, stress management, and learning. Because doing so unlocks your energy, the precious currency that stands between you and a richer, more aligned life.

So, you may be wondering how you can possibly engage with anything new when you're feeling so (insert the blank that fits here) depleted, tired, overwhelmed, or overscheduled. You may also be wondering why energy, the fuel that catapults you closer to your needs, often eludes you. Or why making the time for routines and practices that really work for you doesn't work consistently.

After all, we know what we're "supposed" to do. But, because of what it means to be a mom, in most families it's completely inaccessible. Sadly, seeking "work–life balance" rarely leads to getting more of the right work or life things done. Like the pursuit of callings, delicious stretches of continuous thought, long walks, playing heartily with our kids, or daily rest and recovery. Balance, for most women with families means "more housework" or maybe even "more childcare" but it's usually not the kind of childcare we love, like getting to know our children as people. It's often the mental load of logistics, like planning camps and scheduling appointments. Or shuttling them back and forth to activities and worse, answering more emails about all of these options.

The health erosion that disproportionately affects women with caregiving responsibilities, whether it's moms or eldercare givers, isn't widely discussed. Nor is the all-too-common weathering in the Black community and other underserved communities. Like stones beaten smooth from years of waves, the mental energy we spend navigating systemic racism and sexism becomes an ever-present source of trauma.

Many of us are trying to achieve something our ancestors and own mothers never achieved: you probably want better outcomes for your children—financially, emotionally, and physically—without the same sacrifices of previous generations. I want that, too, for yours and for mine, but the reality is, without awareness of the invisible stressors, an unassailable self-regard, and daily routines that actually work for the unpredictability of motherhood, sustained change will elude us.

And we often go about it the wrong way. We're trained to push harder and work more to please others. Often in environments where we're forced to pretend and ignore our needs like appreciation, transparency, and rest. So we go into this fight, against everything we've ever been taught, exhausted and empty.

What I'm about to share isn't exactly about doing less, because dialing back doesn't map with reality. Women work incredibly hard and women who are caregivers work impossibly hard. And those of us who are also from communities of color, are disabled, or LGBTQ+ spend even more mental energy to achieve what often feels like the bare minimum.

Like you, I live this reality daily. I was drawn to this challenge in part because of my experiences of motherhood and because I've used research to inform growth and innovation strategy for over 20 years. Mom's Hierarchy of Needs began as a passion project and research blog, not a business. I was a committed "corporate girl" and had no intention of leaving my safety salary or family's health insurance behind to leap into business, especially with my kids in remote school as the pandemic raged on. But when I was laid off within a few months of starting a new job it was shortly before COVID hit. I had barely updated my résumé when the global economy went into a free fall. So, I became an entrepreneur by accident. Prior to that, I held leadership positions at some of the world's most admired companies and in the past decade plus, my career has been focused on the children's mental health, children's educational publishing, childcare, eldercare, family technology, and market research industries. I'm a frequent speaker, researcher, and consultant to organizations on how to engage and support parents and caregivers. I'm also a passionate advocate for public policy reform and have been fortunate to use my voice to amplify needs like childcare and eldercare access, paid family leave, domestic workers' rights, and other critical supports for a brighter caregiving future.

I've heard from thousands of women about what's hardest, interviewed hundreds of specialists, and have deconstructed popular advice, mostly from well-intentioned men, who don't keep "mom schedules" about how to be healthy and successful, into the little interventions that work for us. It's not perfect, or easy, but it's achievable and just trying is worth it.

I'm telling you that the trick to all of this is to ruthlessly care for yourself while caring for others. Not to use the Mom's Hierarchy of Needs, as an "oxygen mask you put on first" because that's too simplistic to explain the micro trade-offs we make all day long. But use the awareness, principles, and actions (informed by research, of course) in ways that are highly modular and flexible to suit the dynamic nature of your life.

Because your energy, which disappears when you're overworked, is at the heart of your next promotion, book proposal, board seat, Pulitzer Prize, marathon, inspired family adventure, or just finding a moment of peace.

Whatever "it" looks like for you, that thing you really want to accomplish in this season—without your mental, emotional, and physical energy, it won't happen.

And we all know what the barriers are. My daily work is in systems change—unwinding policies, benefits, and practices of the workplace. But let me tell you something you probably already know. We may become grandparents before the systems of work and US public policies change enough to matter.

If you choose to implement something doable that helps make your life better now rather than wait for "the systems" to be fixed fully, please keep reading. And ditto if you've tried to solve this before unsuccessfully. Because most of us try and fail at least a dozen times.

I wrote this book for moms, but there are structural inequities that disproportionately hurt all historically overlooked groups, like women, people of color, those who are disabled, or LGBTQ+. And if you identify with more than one of these historically marginalized categories, your climb is steeper. Although my post-pandemic research study currently includes 1% nonbinary people, most of the research hasn't caught up to gender fluidity. So, I'll refer to the difficulties faced by people who identify as women and moms.

Moms are already fighting multiple layers of inequity. If like me, you're also a woman of color or from an immigrant family, then you're probably eager to make your life and your children's lives better right now. Because you promised your parents, who had it even harder, that you would. Increasing energy when you've been overlooked, overworked, and underestimated is not an easy thing to do. Especially when you're ambitious and navigating growth, as a person and professionally, at the same time.

But it's essential for your health.

I use what I'm about to teach you in my own life, which is why you're reading this. I burned out when I returned to work from my second maternity leave just over nine years ago, imploding a job I once loved. And having dealt with some difficult circumstances growing up, including going onto food stamps and losing the home I grew up in during middle school, I never imagined I would make bold transitions within my corporate career, in my forties with a baby and a toddler. Nor did I expect to build a movement, and later a business, from an idea.

As a Black woman, whose parents are from the Caribbean, I had a very different path in mind. But this work is my calling, and health for moms is my ministry. And you would have never heard from me or of me if I hadn't emerged from burnout by implementing these systems and changes.

So, I will start with some "myth busting" for the invisible barriers to overcoming the never-done list and making the types of changes you're told that you "should" make. Of course, you should get more sleep, move more, ignore what's outside of your control, and stress less—it's common knowledge.

I probably won't tell you to "do" something you haven't heard of before. I'll help you overcome the reasons it doesn't "stick" for you, or for most people, and honor your brilliance by explaining why. Often, the vague way this information is shared or implemented by others whose lives mostly don't work like yours makes it difficult to learn from.

This book is about using every single tool in your tool kit to make more space for yourself. And I'm not talking about little scraps of space; I'm talking about at least one or more hours each day to do what serves you. For me that was really recovering from burnout, regaining my health, clarity, and changing my career.

But for you it could be something entirely different. You're in a judgment-free zone here. If you want one or two more hours a day so you can sleep more, binge watch *Bridgerton*, eat ice cream, or hang with your friends, awesome. Whatever "it" is, doesn't matter. What you need depends on your season and goals. So, my role here is to help you overcome the barriers to it.

You may be thinking, "Leslie, well my situation is unique because of (insert the blank)." But guess what? Everyone's situation is unique. We don't live cookie-cutter lives yet the core problem is the same.

You don't have much discretionary time, if any. And when you do, you either feel too guilty to use it or you're interrupted 100 times. That's it, right? Okay, I'm here with you and for you. Because that is what we all deal with.

I'm going to help you make more space for yourself so you can invest it in your health, growth, well-being, joy, or whatever it is that you decide to do. And over time you're going to decide to do different things. I'm just going to teach you how to tweak your approach.

I break this down for you into three main sections of the book:

- First, free your mind by understanding how to identify and overcome the most common obstacles to clarity and calm. Like the cognitive load and decision fatigue that can make your brain feel like it's been through a shredder by 10 a.m.
- Next, we have to ease your workload and give you the tools and systems to shift, trim, eliminate, and repeat as often as possible. Not to mention, avoiding the trap of thinking better boundaries are the answer by creating a preemptive plan for the biggest boundary traps we face.

- Then, you get to the good stuff, fuel your future, by unlocking those natural sources of energy that are impossible to tap into until you have more space. You know, health-driven energy, like caring for your body, managing the crushing strain of emotional labor, moving more, and putting great stuff into your body, like nutritious foods.

Context matters. So, we will dig into the why and the how, because that's what makes these updates accessible. The emphasis is on what you can do to put yourself at the top of the Mom's Hierarchy of Needs more often every day, tailored in ways that suit your beautiful life, your goals, and your season.

Sound good? Alright, let's go!

Section One

FREE YOUR MIND

Chapter 1

Escape from the Tunnel

"I'm going for a run outside. Would you like to join me?" he asked. Only in California would every treadmill (about eight of them) be busy at 5 a.m. Seriously, all of the treadmills were in use so I waited while stretching, doing jumping jacks, skipping rope, and then more stretching. On the yoga mat next to me, was a tall, nice-looking man. I learned he was also a runner, because we fell into an easy rapport while waiting for the very popular treadmills to open up.

I laughed, perhaps a bit nervously, "it's a bit too dark for an outdoor run! Isn't it?" He explained that it would be light enough to start soon and because he traveled to this area frequently, he knew a good route that was between five and six miles long.

Like many mornings, when I'm on the other coast the three-hour time difference inevitably meant waking up at 3 or 4 a.m. I thought without my then toddler daughter or active kindergartener son that maybe I would sleep fully. But despite trying valiantly to return to sleep for nearly two hours, it was fruitless. So, I accepted defeat and went down to the gym.

It was a business trip hotel morning and my meetings would start in a few hours. At first, I demurred while thinking, "of course, I can't go running with you through the dark streets of Los Angeles; I don't know you!" Even though I was in Southern California and love to run outside—at 5 a.m. it was a rather cold, dark place. Not conducive to running in the lightweight, indoor gear I packed. And, of course, there was the other matter: running in an unfamiliar place with a complete stranger.

"We'll never get a treadmill," he explained. I glanced at the treadmill runners, and based on their steady, intense gaits, and how they were dressed they were clearly committed athletes with no intention of leaving their posts anytime soon. "Okay, I'd love to join you. I just need to run upstairs for a sweatshirt," The words came out of my mouth before I could think about the implications too much. "Great!" He beamed a big smile, "why don't you meet me at the front door in 10 minutes?"

When I got outside, I half-wondered if I had completely lost my mind. He waved and I realized how very tall, and strong he was now that we were both standing up. How I'd be out, in the near-dark with this man who could easily overpower me. How on the surface, it didn't seem very safe or wise but, for some reason I went anyway. And as the sun came up behind the California hills, amidst the palm trees, I was grateful that I did. It was breathtaking. And in those five-and-a-half mostly quiet miles, I learned about my running mate's kids, divorce, hometown in the Midwest, and that he happened to work for the same large media company I was in town to meet with.

This was in March 2017. Less than four months after the most toxic US election cycle I had experienced, and the loss of my stepson, I felt empty. And exhausted from checking every box when the world around me felt so broken. I was sick of the programming that I was supposed to subscribe to, that I should fear versus embrace other people. I was also tired of the pleasing, accommodating, hypervigilance, and self-sacrifice that was expected of me. Especially when it only seemed to make life easier for everyone else. So, shivering in that Universal City parking lot, it didn't matter that I was wearing light shorts and a tank top under a thin sweatshirt and it was only 45 degrees. Or that I was about to go running with a stranger. I just wanted to break free. And feel the exhilaration of trusting my own instincts and trusting others, even if it was just for a little while.

You were probably taught, like most of us were, to fear the unknown. Unknown paths and unknown people. But when following every rule, while trying to live the everywoman life, leaves you feeling flat, what do you do? When you feel powerless from all of that compliance, how do you recharge?

It's probably not by digging deeper into the never-done list or retreating from yourself. And it's probably not by holding the lid of the box, the one we're all expected to fit into as mothers, tightly over your dreams and desires.

When you want more than what society gives us, like space to breathe, think, and create, what you want, and richly deserve, is more time at the top of the Mom's Hierarchy of Needs®. Because it's your birthright as a human being to care for yourself. Don't worry, we're going to get right into the details of what this means for you over the next couple of pages.

No, You Are Not Imagining It

You've probably heard the term *the motherhood penalty*, which is a well-researched acknowledgment of the financial hit we take from the combination of lost wages, promotions, and career growth after having kids. By contrast, men receive a "fatherhood bonus" and make more money for each child they have.

But the motherhood penalty isn't just about the money. Or even career advancement. Yes, it's the main reason for the wage and leadership gaps for women but it's also at the heart of the health gap. Because motherhood is so poorly supported, especially here in the United States, we're not only professionally and financially undermined, we pay a steep tax with our mental and physical health.

Let me explain, because this issue—health for moms—is at the heart of my ministry. It's what drives me to do this work and why you are reading this book. Many of us find ourselves slowly drifting into a tunnel we don't emerge from, for years, if ever.

Because to make "more time" in the day, moms tend to pause or remove activities at the top of the Mom's Hierarchy of Needs first (see Figure 1.1). The activities that support our mental, physical, and emotional health, such as healthy adult relationships and, yes, that includes your partner if you have one; self-care, which in my paradigm includes sleep, stress management, movement, and nutrition; also learning, fun, interests, and growth.

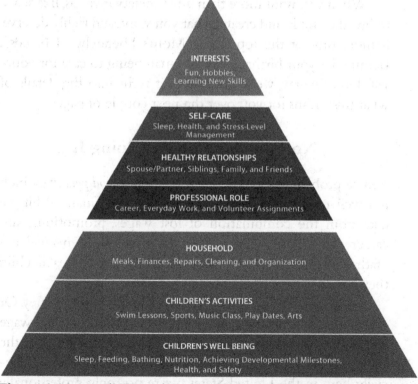

Figure 1.1 Mom's Hierarchy of Needs framework.

The reason we don't get to the top of the Mom's Hierarchy of Needs very often is because the activities in the bottom two-thirds that we cherish and prioritize, like our children's milestones, education, and well-being, or our household roles and professional responsibilities, are never done. And before kids, it's common to think, "well, when everything I have to do is done then I will" (insert the blank that fits for you here). Go for that walk, call that friend, pursue that PhD, whatever "it" is doesn't matter. It continues to get hurled over the edge of to-do-list mountain.

Accordioning to McKinsey's Future of Wellness report,[1] last year the industry was worth $1.8 trillion, with the United States coming in at $480 billion of that. Yep . . . billion. However, we are left out of the wellness conversation, even though the industry profits from our desperation to "feel better" and "get healthy." Women are courted for everything from weight loss, anti-aging, shiny hair, and comfortable shoes. But among men and those with a lot of resources—okay, mostly it's the men with a lot of resources—the conversation has shifted. It's all about health span now. Maximizing the healthy years, by not only optimizing for longevity but also clarity and productivity in the most human sense, not the workplace sense, of the word.

The truth is caregiving makes creating healthy routines really hard. The increasing volume of both expected and unplanned demands on our mental, physical, and emotional energy, combined with less and less access to discretionary time, becomes its own slow-acting poison on our well-being. Many books address the underlying issue of time famine, which disproportionately affects women in different ways. Motherly's[2] *2024 State of Motherhood Report* cites that just 39% of moms surveyed between the ages of 18 and 43 get at least an hour to themselves each day. Not only is that a sad statistic but it's also been validated in many other studies with time use data. Sadder still is that most women do not even get an hour per day. Okay, you're probably not surprised, because you live some flavor of this or see it in those around you.

If you have less than an hour per day to yourself, where do you fit in movement, cultivating healthy adult relationships—like with your partner (if you are partnered) or friends, siblings, or parents? Not to mention stress management, learning, or nutritious meals? You can't even watch a movie or get a decent haircut within that window! So, pause for a moment to think about the implications. And how not having enough time for self-care, which includes rest, ripples through our lives in devastating ways.

> "99% of my time goes to these three things: work, childcare, housework. I feel like I'm always rushing from one to the other, although they're essentially all happening at once. When I'm not dead exhausted I do 30 minutes of forced exercise bc I would lose my mind without it. But it feels like I'm stealing from those three other things or from MUCH needed relaxation every time I do it. I wish there was a way to either work fewer hours or have some child care or something so I can have some self-care."

This and the following are anonymous quotes from the Mom's Hierarchy of Needs pandemic study where over 3,700 parents, mostly mothers (98%) have shared their stories since March 30, 2020. I began this study to understand what was happening, having no idea how long it would run for, but I knew it would be epic. I didn't realize how large it would get but early on, I hired a former market research colleague and talented data consultant with a master's in public health to assist with the analysis. It's the longest running study of its kind about how the pandemic, and now post-pandemic, conditions continue to affect work–life balance, health, support needs, and priorities. And one thing is clear: moms feel imprisoned by society's unrealistic expectations and declining workplace trust. We realize that trying to follow the hidden rules telling us how to raise kids, care for our bodies, partners, homes, and careers isn't sustainable.

> "There's no immediate consequences to depriving myself care, but if my kids or job or house needs are not met right away, there are major consequences immediately. And more stress for me."

Perhaps not surprisingly, across every wave of the study, all of the self-care dimensions measured are way down because our workloads and life's complexity has increased and remains high. Moms felt the most confident overall in their parenting when the study began, because our children were with us 24/7 but as the children's mental health crisis and academic slide grew, parenting confidence declined. Only 30% of those who are married or coupled feel like they're doing "as well" or "better" in their partnerships, a statistic that hasn't really improved throughout the study.

> "We have 3 kids and no village."

Most moms can't care for their basic well-being, let alone their growth. A significant number of moms in our study say self-care is "showering" and "eating regularly," and, no, these are not just the moms of newborns! But society's messages continue to tell us we can have more than this, and worse, it appears possible until you try. But everyone has reexamined their priorities post-COVID and mothers, perhaps more than ever, are looking for better answers. The first Mom's Hierarchy of Needs research study to sleuth out the reasons behind the stress was in 2017 and, sadly, not much has changed. Although everyone started talking about "the new normal" post-pandemic, it turns out that moms hated the "old normal" with its express demands to be "on" all of the time and inability to attend to our most basic needs.

Whether moms are in the paid workforce, partnered, privileged, or none of those things, they still lack time[3] and energy[4] to care for their mental, physical, and emotional health, everything at the top of the Mom's Hierarchy of Needs.

In the most recent wave of our post-pandemic research study, 79% of surveyed moms cite doing "terribly" or "not as well as usual" at self-care. And they continue to lose their confidence and sense of self-efficacy, in their most important roles—as parents, partners, workers, and caregivers to themselves. And in case you're wondering, it's worse now (a 19-point slide) than in spring 2020. Really. Self-care routines, like movement,[5] sleep, and stress management[6] give us energy for the marathon of parenting,[7] partnering,[8] and career building.[9] So, what stands in the way?

Let's Start with the Capacity Challenge

> "[I have] absolutely no time. Little help with a 5-month-old, no maternity leave, expensive childcare, absence of formula and medical debt after a c section."

When asked about the barriers to self-care, more than a third (38%) of surveyed moms, from this same Mom's Hierarchy of Needs study, cite insufficient childcare[10] (29%) and support[11] (9%) for doing all the things. One in four (25%) directly credits lack of time. This is followed by struggles with their health[12] (14%), including mental health,[13] mood (yep, that includes guilt[14]), and difficulty setting boundaries[15] (9%).

Although moms are the default doers in most homes, the post-pandemic economic and social[16] climate have ramped up life's complexity and emotional weight in excruciating ways. With the global conflicts, record inflation, and decreased spending power, we also face shortages for childcare, teachers, and children's mental health providers. So, when asked what are the biggest barriers to your self-care or well-being, they had a lot to say.

Everything Is Harder, and It Was Hard Before

"I have a 2-year-old, I'm in a custody battle, I have a stalker, I don't make enough money to be independent despite being in management and having my degree, I have little free time outside of work, I am depressed, I have complex post-traumatic stress disorder, I am pregnant."

Moms lack sufficient childcare, mental health care, and support playing multiple roles, which leads to less time, money, and resources to prioritize ourselves. So, most face declining physical health and energy, often while our children and partners thrive. And the systemic changes that would influence our daily lives remain elusive or hotly debated by legislators.

Dr. Vivek Murty, the former US Surgeon General, issued an advisory report warning that parent stress is a public health emergency. Yes, you read that right, the office of the Surgeon General of these United States, the same office that has previously issued public health warnings about social media for teens, and smoking, has elevated parenting in our current climate to a health hazard. The report includes data that echoes what I have and will continue to share, from my studies and others. Including the following: ". . . 41% of parents say that most days they are so stressed they cannot function and 48% say that most days their stress is completely overwhelming compared to other adults (20% and 26%, respectively)."

"I want to find a way to be happier, less stressed, less anxious—and therefore be a better mother."

The report mostly uses the gender-neutral term *parenting* but acknowledges parents who are in historically marginalized groups, like women and people of color, those who are disabled, LGBTQ+, have food or housing instability, are divorced, or experience violence are affected disproportionately by these stressors. Knowing what I know about the data behind this report and others like it, we're overwhelmingly talking about the plight of moms here. The mental health of fathers, as acknowledged in the Surgeon General's report, have been less studied. All of this echoes many of the themes in our research and what I've been preaching for the past seven-plus years, because, of course, none of this is new.

Caregiver burnout is a known cause of health disparities and can refer to nonparents, like those working in the medical field caring for others, or the impact on family caregivers, which many of us are by also caring for adults such as our parents. But before dismissing the data as the "same old mom martyrdom" song we've been singing most of our lives, there is something new and important to pay attention to. Life after a pandemic is still pretty novel. And that major event altered and destabilized critical infrastructure parents and caregivers rely on—such as the childcare, eldercare, health care, and education industries.

The weight of seeing the Surgeon General's report only underscores the urgency and need for change. Which is awesome. But even though most of my work is on the systems change side, I won't get too into the weeds of it for the purpose of this book. Because this book is about you, and what you can do, despite how messed up our systems are. So, let's get back to you, shall we?

Is it safe to assume you're unwilling to wait for the systems to catch up to the decades of data? Okay, same. I mean, really smart women have been writing about these problems since the 1950s and 1960s. It's painful but we're at a cultural inflection point. Pain leads to change, and we get to choose certain aspects of our paths. But you need the tools and the will to choose yourself and find a route, pace, and approach that serves you.

So, here's a quick peek at what's happening:

- Fifty-three percent of women in 2024 say they're more stressed[17] than a year ago and 46% say they're burned out.
- Nearly half (48%) of employed mothers in our pandemic study are less committed to their jobs.
- More working mothers (aka, in the paid workforce, since all mothers work really hard) have been diagnosed with anxiety and/or depression[18] (42%) than the general population (28%), their coworkers without kids (25%), and even working fathers (35%). Working mothers were also more likely to report that their mental health had worsened in the last year (33%).

Which Only Obscures Your Path

Every mom is sitting on some wonderful idea that can change her life or the world, and she's either too tired, fearful, or time constrained to implement it. We worry the dreams we held for our adult selves are becoming increasingly invisible. And the "mom box" everyone wants to put us in is so full of self-sacrifice and overwork that there isn't room for our unique voices to be heard.

We reluctantly dismiss, diminish, and hide our talents as we conform to society's belief that women should be humble, unseen, and seldom truly heard. But there is a Mom's Hierarchy of Needs. And you can use this as a flexible foundation to help transform your daily life and get closer to your deepest human needs. But to do so, we need to emerge from under the glare of the massive gaslight.

So, what really stands between you and your well-being (hint, it's not your willpower)?

"Your blood pressure is quite high. Is that normal for you?" I looked over at the nurse, still wondering if I'd be home in time for my next meeting. "No, it's always been low." I quickly added, "But in a healthy way, not too low. It's never been a problem." She handed me a cotton gown, more tarp than clothing, and said, "Please leave the opening in the back. The doctor will be in shortly."

I thanked her and quickly undressed. Once the gown was on, I took a few deep breaths from the end of the exam table. I tried to lie back, thinking, maybe I would just rest for a minute. But between the cold room and breezy gown, it wasn't exactly comfortable. So, after a few minutes I got up to retrieve my laptop, confident I could manage at least a couple of emails when the door opened. "Hi, Leslie! It's great to see you." I absolutely love my primary care doctor. "It's great to see you, too! Thank you for fitting me in."

She started reading the notes from my conversation with the nurse and asked, "So, tell me about your headaches, Leslie. How long has it been?"

I said, "It's been at least a month . . . okay perhaps a bit longer than that to be honest. I thought about coming in earlier, but I just hoped it would go away. I don't normally get headaches, but it's been so busy and, well, you know." She gave me a look because years before, I admitted that although I love seeing her, I really don't like to see doctors unless it's an emergency. It's mostly from growing up with a Bajan Mom who had a home remedy for every malady we faced as kids. I could almost hear Mum's voice inside of my head. "Les, hurt your knee? Have some sugar water. Cut your hand? Let's get some aloe. Stomach ache? I'll make some ginger tea."

My doctor said, "I'd like to take your blood pressure again." As the cuff on my arm tightened, I tried to think calm thoughts. Barbados thoughts. I pictured myself swimming gently on my back through the warm water as I had hundreds of times before. I imagined the sounds of the distant jet skis and waves . . . . "Leslie, it's still reading very high." So much for the visualization I thought.

She asked, "What does the headache feel like?" I replied, "It feels like I'm wearing a ponytail too tight and it's pretty much constant now."

"Okay, well high blood pressure can cause headaches. But so can a lot of other things. Well, let's talk about your diet." My eyes lit up because food, making it, cooking it, and talking about it was my jam. "I cook almost every day and I don't eat processed food unless I'm somewhere where it's the only option, like an airport. I make all of my children's snacks and bread. I eat greens every night, even when I'm traveling. But I do have a sweet tooth and will pick up a cookie after lunch sometimes."

"Well, treats here and there aren't a problem." She frowned slightly. "Can you take a deep breath? And hold it please. I don't think your diet is an issue." She added, "What about alcohol, how often do you drink?"

"I'm still nursing, so it's less now. But I love wine and usually have a glass or two most nights. Sometimes more."

She was taking notes. "How much more?"

I sighed and said, "it depends." I didn't want to be evasive but I wasn't thrilled about the idea of losing the only vice I had left either.

"Are you still running regularly?"

"Yes, every day, somewhere between two and four miles; it depends on how much time I have."

"Okay, well let's talk about stress." I laughed. "Okay, where do you want to start?"

"Seriously, Leslie. Tell me about work. Are you still traveling a lot?" She and I hadn't seen each other since my annual checkup, at least six months before. "Sort of, I'm in a new job which means less long-distance travel, but my job is in New York."

"So, that's quite the commute from Boston, how often are you there?" she asked. I explained, "Because I'm still new, it's every week while I'm learning. I spend a few days in New York and one day in the Boston office. Then I'm home on Fridays. Although it's tough with the baby and pumping. I negotiated a four-day week, which is wonderful. At least, it was in the beginning . . . ." My voice trailed off as my thoughts returned to my current situation.

I felt so comfortable with her, that my real worries spilled out. "Because I'm traveling there every week, I'm spending a lot of extra money on childcare. When I took this job, I thought it was okay to take a big pay cut because my husband was making more. But he was laid off over the summer. So, I'm under a lot of financial strain." She said with a sigh, "Are you doing anything other than exercise to manage the stress?"

I explained that despite having gone through an intensive meditation and cognitive course before my oldest was born, there was barely room for the running I managed to fit. We also discussed drinking water, something I was sporadic about, largely so I wouldn't have to pee as much during the workday. She said, "Well with all the exercise you're doing, and breast-feeding, you need to drink more than 8 cups a day, probably more like 10 or 12. Let's see if that helps because being dehydrated can cause headaches, too. But just in case, I'd like you to take your blood pressure at home for the next couple of weeks and then come back in to see me. You can buy a blood pressure monitor at any drugstore."

"Okay. I can do that but . . . I doubt it's my blood pressure." At that point, I was perplexed. And completely wrong. Sure, I was still exercising every day, cooking and eating mostly nutritious foods, but it wasn't enough. This was in late October of 2015, shortly after downshifting into a job that was supposed to give me more space to recover from burning out in the previous job. Although I desperately searched for a way to make my life and work, fit together, I was still exhausted. I thought sleep was an "every mom" challenge I needed to just deal with and felt the same way about my stress, which was off the charts by then. The reality was, I pretty much abandoned time for myself unless it was exercise, especially in the form of rest, hobbies, or enjoyment.

What Have You Stopped Doing?

You've probably given up some self-care anchors after becoming a mom. Remember the Mom's Hierarchy of Needs framework? The time that you pour into your priorities as a mother in those bottom two-thirds of the triangle, like your children's well-being has to come from somewhere. After all, your life was probably pretty full before. So, inevitably we will trade off our self-care categories, like exercise, sleep, and our friendship time. The lack of restorative activities to counteract the new demands can trigger the extreme stress rollercoaster. Why? Well, even if you were taking amazing care of yourself just the physical transitions we experience put new strain on our minds and bodies. Whether it's the hormonal ups and downs of pregnancy or fertility treatments, the postpartum phase, or perimenopause. Then, of course there are the sleep disruptions through each one, and in the backdrop for many, the extra effort it takes to rise in our careers. But women are already at greater risk for a whole lot of stress-related illnesses, such as anxiety, depression, and autoimmune diseases. And for women of color, the stats are generally worse. So, how much pushing through can we really tolerate?

Okay, so I'm sure I have your attention now, and I'm telling you this because I wish someone told me these things, nine years ago when my daughter was born. Or perhaps even sooner, like before my son was born. But we all stop doing something, or many, many somethings, for our preventative health or growth after having kids. We don't have predictable or sufficient discretionary time. Yet, we're socialized to feel guilty about using what little time we do have when we have it.

I will continue to sing this, like an anthem, throughout the book. And if I've seen any consistency about the challenges we face to our health, happiness, and career growth, from the thousands of moms who have participated in my research studies, it's that self-care activities are the first to go. Let me be clear, when I refer to "self-care" it's meant as Audre Lorde, the scholar and poet who coined the term intended. She said, "Caring for myself is not self-indulgence, it is self-preservation and that is an act of political warfare." Yep, that's right. So, choosing self-care is a "radical act" in a world that doesn't value it for us. Which means, we need to fiercely protect it for ourselves.

Remember that story about my doctor's visit? Well, at that point although I didn't feel good, I thought I was "super healthy" because I was able to fit into my skinny jeans. But a few weeks later, she confirmed that I did in fact have high blood pressure, also known as the "silent killer" of women. If I hadn't had the headaches, or seen my doctor about them, who knows what might have happened. I was under so much stress that I wasn't managing well. I always thought of myself as a healthy person and didn't know that everything I held dear was at risk. So, after the diagnosis, I had to question my assumptions. And look back to when the stress became relentless.

Let's check back with you. How are you feeling? This is your call to action to not only have your regular checkups (something we'll cover in Section Three in greater depth) but also to go in and make that health care appointment when you don't feel well. Ensure that you are seen, stay attentive about any follow-up visits, and ask every question you have if you're unclear about the medical advice you receive. I'm lucky I have a great doctor who listens, but if you don't, see someone else. Remember, in the same way you would wrestle a medical need to the ground like a bear on behalf of your children, it's critical to do the same for yourself. That's not just the physical needs either, because constant worry, unhappiness, exhaustion, and lack of sleep are very real health problems that require the same immediate attention as a fall or an injury.

Notes

1. https://www.mckinsey.com/industries/consumer-packaged-goods/our-insights/the-trends-defining-the-1-point-8-trillion-dollar-global-wellness-market-in-2024
2. https://www.mother.ly/news/2024-state-of-motherhood-report/
3. https://momshierarchyofneeds.com/2021/08/28/why-yes-its-that-time-time-to-regain-control-of-your-time/
4. https://momshierarchyofneeds.com/2022/07/02/want-real-independence-strategies-for-a-guilt-free-life-full-of-energy/
5. https://momshierarchyofneeds.com/2018/05/02/strong-fit-resilient-get-motivated-make-it-happen/
6. https://momshierarchyofneeds.com/2021/05/01/trapped-in-the-stress-cycle-take-back-your-mental-health-at-home/
7. https://momshierarchyofneeds.com/2018/07/10/can-mindfulness-modeling-overcome-impatience-from-the-mental-load/
8. https://momshierarchyofneeds.com/2018/03/29/ask-for-more-the-roadmap-to-equal-partnership-at-home/
9. https://momshierarchyofneeds.com/2021/04/24/leadership-without-burnout-how-to-build-your-capacity-and-energy/

10. https://momshierarchyofneeds.com/2021/02/07/are-you-weighing-your-childcare-options-right-now/
11. https://momshierarchyofneeds.com/2022/01/22/conquer-those-self-limiting-beliefs-with-the-right-support/
12. https://momshierarchyofneeds.com/2021/10/30/its-healthy-to-take-breaks-when-youre-exhausted-heres-how-to-pause/
13. https://momshierarchyofneeds.com/2022/02/26/what-alternatives-do-you-have-to-get-mental-health-support/
14. https://momshierarchyofneeds.com/2021/10/16/can-you-escape-the-relentless-strain-of-mom-guilt-on-your-life/
15. https://momshierarchyofneeds.com/2019/02/21/how-can-moms-set-boundaries-without-feeling-guilty/
16. https://momshierarchyofneeds.com/2020/11/01/the-elections-are-you-hopeful-or-discouraged/
17. https://www2.deloitte.com/content/dam/Deloitte/global/Documents/deloitte-women-at-work-2022-a-global-outlook.pdf
18. https://www.cvshealth.com/news/mental-health/the-mental-health-crisis-of-working-moms.html

Chapter 2

See the Three Ghosts for What They Are

"We're sorry, Leslie, but we're letting you go," my colleague said quietly. He didn't have to say it because when he and my boss entered the room together, I knew. At this point, there was a recession and a lot of people had already been laid off from my then employer, including quite a few friends, people I loved and relied on. But I thought I was safe, after opening our first office in China.

I was the company's crown jewel because at the time, China was where the growth was among our global client base. I made that happen, with my infant son in tow for all of the overseas trips, and now that it was done, they were letting me go?

Even looking back, I remember how dislocated that conversation felt. I know I pushed back on the timing when they told me it was only two weeks of transition. Their words were swallowed up, almost like I was standing next to an airplane about to take off. I countered with everything I could to create more time, which meant more income. I remember saying, "But I can't wrap up my projects and transition in two weeks.

How about a month at least? What about our partner in China, I need to tell her personally." They proceeded to tell me that they were transitioning my responsibilities for the international part of my job to a colleague who had never been outside of the United States. Not ever. I wasn't sad or angry, I was just stunned. Stunned because of my huge accomplishments in China only a few months before. Stunned because a few weeks before that I excitedly confided in my boss about my pregnancy. And then, shortly after, miscarriage.

The layoff meeting was on my first Monday back after what was supposed to be a mini-vacation. We took a long weekend to see my husband's family in San Diego, and I intended to decompress. But my then boss, and our CEO who was my boss' boss, called me throughout the trip. I would be holding my toddler son in one hand, on the beach, with my other hand pressing the phone to my ear to hear my colleagues above the sounds of crashing waves. This was before my daughter was born and at the time, I felt drained for many reasons: in part, because of my over-the-top work ethic and reluctance to take time off. But I was on a very high-profile project with tight deadlines since I came back to work from maternity leave with my first, almost two years before. And at that stage of my career, despite my seniority, I never set any work–life boundaries. I took pride in being sought after and responsive. So, I encouraged people to reach out to me with questions if they were time sensitive. Yet, that last, pre-layoff long weekend was filled with work interruptions. And it was the last break I had before I started to lose my mind over losing my job.

Notice When Something Breaks

In the year before my son was born, my relationship to work became fractured. I was slowly marginalized in ways few could see. The company, bigger and more political, became openly competitive. It was the kind of below-the-surface-warfare I retreat from. The slippery slide from grace only accelerated after my son was born. At that point, I didn't understand this wasn't just my experience. According to the *Harvard Business Review*, 43% of mothers pause or end their careers for caregiving because making it work, with paid work, is so hard. Or that, one in five experience pregnancy bias[1] and 23% are pushed out of their jobs. I also didn't understand how I was already a rarity. A Black woman in a senior leadership role, in a public company, was about as common as seeing a Faberge egg. I didn't think about how all of that "otherness" I had going on would change my career trajectory. I just clung to my corporate life like the security blanket it was.

I went away to heal from the physical and emotional drain of being pregnant and then not. At the time, I needed more than anything to rest but losing my job, in a recession no less, started a different kind of downward spiral. If you lack generational wealth or grow up with financial instability, like I did, a job is like air. And suddenly, I felt like I was suffocating.

Do you give yourself time to think, and reflect on what feels either really aligned or really off in your life? It may take you a while to just give yourself some space where you are not committed to helping, serving, supporting, feeding, bathing, toileting, or otherwise managing other people. And I'm not just talking about your kids, I'm talking about everybody.

So, getting clear is step number one. We'll spend more time together on exactly how to do that too, starting in Chapter 3. Because once you're clear you can really start to frame up what you want in this season of your motherhood journey.

Begin to Ask Yourself Questions

You're going to need to figure out what you're afraid of. There were so many things that I was afraid of that made this part of the journey, from self-sacrifice to self-care longer than it needed to be, and until I really understood them, I couldn't move forward. I had a complicated childhood, including financial instability, starting when I was about 11 years old. I was afraid of thinking about it or navigating how that shaped my adult choices, including my career, for a long time.

So, if you're spinning in circles, with your parenting, career, perhaps also while caring for your parents, and otherwise navigating the swirl in real time, it discourages reflection. Because of course, that requires the quiet time you rarely get. But think of where you can pause, for little three-, four-, or five-minute stretches of empty space to breathe and think. Many years ago, I interviewed Christine Koh, a multitalented entrepreneur who intentionally put five minutes onto her calendar before the start of each meeting for deep breathing. In another wonderful interview, psychologist and anxiety specialist Dr. Caroline Danda, PhD, advised noticing your transitions throughout the day and taking one or two minutes to be mindful for each one. So, before you get up from your computer and head into the kitchen, or leave the playground with your kids, notice and take a quick breath.

What is easiest for you? What feels hardest? Who can help you? Because you're going to need help; everybody does. It doesn't mean you need to hire a personal coach or a therapist to navigate your transformation, although if you can, absolutely you should do those things. But it might mean you need to engage with a community such as the fabulous virtual one at Mom's Hierarchy of Needs for some support with whatever "it" is. But this can also be your friends, your neighbors, or an ambitious coworker who has similar goals and interests. I'm planting seeds here for you to start thinking about the type of people you want to surround yourself with. You don't have to have that planned out now; in Section Two, we will dive deeper into the support systems that can help.

Because Your Well-Being Awaits You

By the way, your well-life doesn't necessarily look like mine or your neighbor's. You always get to choose what serves you and adapt. So, a quick reminder on how you can use the Mom's Hierarchy of Needs to reorient your priorities and schedule (see Figure 2.1).

The goal here is for you, to spend time up in the top one-third of the categories, the activities that help reduce the stress hormone (cortisol) in your body and promote better mental, physical, and emotional well-being, like sleep, stress management, learning, interests, and healthy adult relationships every day. Okay, I get it . . . daily sounds like a lot but it doesn't have to be huge blocks of time. It absolutely has to be some amount of your time, okay? Don't worry, we'll work on how you can do this as we progress through the book. In the bottom categories that we cherish or prioritize the most, like our children's milestones, activities, health care, and even household responsibilities like cleaning, meals, and bill paying, the goal is for you to get more help and create systems to streamline the workload to what you consider the most vital at any given time.

Here's a little inspiration from the original Mom's Hierarchy of Needs manifesto, an evolution from the main themes in the earliest research studies:

- We can lift each other up. We can get crafty and reexamine every false assumption to squeeze more discretionary time from our days and reinvest our energy into what fires us up and will change our lives for the better.
- We can begin to see all of the changes we roll with, naturally, in mom-land as point of advantage. Not just pride. We can harness this inner strength to do whatever serves us.
- We can learn to unlock our talents and realize our potential with less stress, guilt, and more inner peace. This time

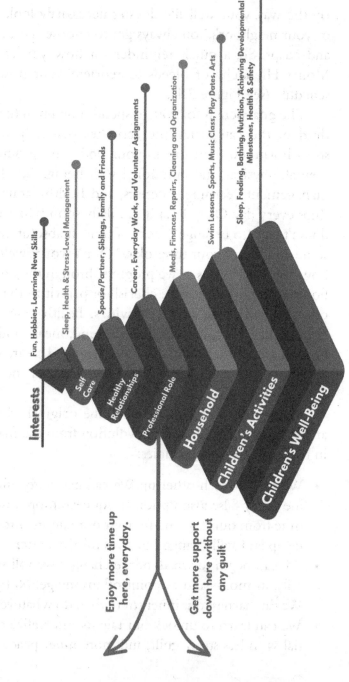

Figure 2.1 How to use the Mom's Hierarchy of Needs framework.

has to be carved out and there are countless moms doing exactly that. We can do it, too.
- We are capable of finding the shortcuts to getting healthier, happier, smarter, stronger, and more secure, emotionally and financially.
- We can put ourselves and our well-being onto the agenda every day, which is great for us and our families.

How does that feel to you? Okay, it might seem like I'm talking about the land of make-believe here but I assure you, I'm not. Although we all feel the strain from daily life, some days more than others, remember you are in community with the most powerful people on the planet: mothers.

How Can You Possibly Restart?

This is the fun part. When you are deeply aware that most of your time is spent thinking about and doing, what are by definition "never-done" things, many of which don't serve you or your family, then you become free to create space for yourself. Yep, big calendar blocks of space to care for you. Your health, your growth, your career, and your relationships, especially the relationship with yourself. After all, can your counters ever be clean forever? Of course not. Will the socks or blocks get picked up off the floor permanently? Is someone judging the space between your couch cushions? No, of course not. So, fretting about all of these chores doesn't make your days any brighter. Years ago, I read some excellent advice, and I wish I remembered the original source. I believe this was a quote in Oprah's magazine but the person in question (whom I remain grateful to for sharing her wisdom) basically said that she evaluates whether a decision will matter in 10 days, 1 year, or 10 years. So, I love clean counters and clean everything for that matter but I'm the only person in my home who feels this way. Spinning myself into knots to continually pick up after other people was only draining my internal batteries and would not matter in 10 days. The counters are perpetually a problem . . . I'm not the only one who uses the kitchen. Concerning myself with teaching my children to read, managing their nutrition, and how to navigate moral dilemmas will matter in 10 years. So, I'm good with investing my time in ways that will have a long-term benefit for my children or even my husband versus fixating on the exhausting and very long list of things that by definition require constant attention yet don't matter that much.

Clearly, I didn't start there, I had to hit some pretty low lows to realize I needed changes. But you are closer than ever to realizing your health and growth goals. And even though the systems we live and work in, like K–12 schools ending mid-afternoon and the lack of protected paid leave, generally work against us, you don't have to tumble off the professional or health cliff to do so.

Yes, They're Real . . . the Ghosts That Conspire to Drain You

Hazel. I kept reading the name, over and over, in hopes it would spark something. After an hour-long meeting, her name was the only note I made. Usually, I take pages of notes for any meeting but this one was different. I was tired and distracted. In part, because my son sent me a series of texts about something that happened at school part-way through the meeting. I knew I needed to reach out to Hazel today but I couldn't remember why. That thought, even though it was part of a discussion I had with 10 other people, completely disappeared. "Excuse me, Leslie, she won't eat the oatmeal. Can I give her something else?" I looked up at the babysitter and sighed. With a deep sense of dread, I followed her into the kitchen. The questions continued, like steady rain, throughout the day. Just when a thought would take hold, a new need like finding a bathing suit, assembling a sippy cup, or providing directions to the park, would surface.

Three days in, I wanted to quit. Abandon the plan and just take the remaining time off. Two and a half weeks ago, I learned our nanny's husband needed major surgery. Unplanned and scary surgery. So, she needed time off to care for him. Although I considered taking all of my remaining vacation time, my company was in the midst of a reorganization. And I was responsible for an unwieldy project. Being on point at work always felt important to me but right then, it felt more so. The project was high profile, and I was on the hot seat. Okay, maybe it was more like a hot oven. Seriously, I was being publicly shamed during meetings at that point about how off the rails the project was. It didn't matter that all of the big decisions that influenced its success, like when it would launch or the profit margins, were already made before I even started. Whether it was fair for me to be on the hot seat or not wasn't the issue. I was experiencing some reorg post-traumatic stress disorder based on past jobs so, any threat to my career felt like an emergency. At the time, my salary was our primary one. So, hiring back-up babysitters seemed like a good plan.

Two hours earlier, I introduced another new sitter to my children. She was the third, from my employer's back-up care service, in less than two weeks. I gave her a quick overview of what needed to happen in the morning, while finishing the breakfast-to-school scramble with my oldest. He was not eating his oatmeal while explaining to me, with my phone in his hands, what the weather would be like for the next week. In detail. One of his nicknames at home is *weatherman* because, well, he's always loved everything about the weather. I started thinking about what clothes to put out for him while giving the sitter instructions on what to put in the diaper bag for my youngest. As I explained the need for sunscreen, a snack pack, towel, and change of clothes, I lobbed another verbal warning at my son to finish. After dropping him off at school, I rushed home to walk the babysitter and my daughter part of the way to the park. I hastily gave directions while checking the time, I had less than 10 minutes to be on my first conference call. I was working from home, because leaving my children with an unfamiliar caregiver made me a bit queasy, and I knew they'd have questions. Although I had no idea how many questions! In that moment, managing the small army of cheerful, yet unfamiliar teen sitters, while trying to stay focused on work was surprisingly stressful. Eventually I remembered the notes. But it took me a full four hours before I could recall why I needed to talk with Hazel.

Two weeks before this, our dryer was broken for three weeks, turning the routine of laundry into a Herculean effort. Think clothing, sheets, and towels draped over every square inch of space in our condo to air-dry 24/7 for weeks. The intense time at my job was matched by the intensity of the housework. So, having a nanny means I usually had someone to help with a lot of the housework during the workweek. But with the back-up babysitters, no housework was done. They didn't even clean up the kids' dishes from their snacks. I was miserable and exhausted but like most times in my life, when I faced a challenge, I thought the answer was to just work harder.

What happens when your already too-long-list becomes even longer? You may be tempted to just dive deeper into getting "it all" done but again, by definition many of these tasks, especially cleaning, have no finish line. I'll repeat, *no finish line*. You may start to feel like you're being pulled into quicksand with an ever-deepening to-do list threatening to swallow your peace. However, hold tight because we're going to discuss the mindset side of this next and why it's so hard to escape.

Meet Ghost Number One: Time Scarcity

We tend to rock a bit of pride as moms when we channel our inner magicians to pull those impossible rabbits, from even more improbable hats. And, yes, there are some upsides from being forced to operate with limited resources, like being able to hyperfocus on our children's needs. But it turns out scarcity of any kind—in this case the time kind—also comes with pretty significant downsides. Like, having it be a continuous invisible drain on our mental bandwidth.

You've probably heard about "scarcity thinking"[2] or "scarcity mindset." it's what happens if you focus on what you don't have. Yes, that can easily get into the mix when we're dealing with time scarcity but I'm referring to something a bit different and larger. In the book *Scarcity, Why Having Too Little Means So Much* authors Sendhil Mullainathan and Eidar Shafir share research on all types of scarcity. But interestingly, whether they researched the lack of food, money, or time, they learned that the natural consequences were consistent. So, they share in the book that the other side of "hyperfocus" that can help us meet deadlines and get things done like the brilliant, time-bending genies we are is developing tunnel vision for problems in ways that obscure the ability to see or react to what's around us. Basically, as they describe the research studies behind the book, some of which I had read previously, scarcity leads to having less "fluid intelligence" therefore, we have "less mind" to problem-solve with. In addition to potentially becoming more impulsive, because resisting temptations like sticking to your diet or even your boundaries requires mental energy.

Sound familiar? So, let's use the example of forgetting about what I agreed to do, during that conference call, which I would probably describe as a mental load issue in that moment, and we'll discuss that more soon. Candidly, slogging through that whole day in the way that I did with the poor results I received wasn't just about forgetting one of the things I needed to do at work. That was only part of the broader problem of dealing with time scarcity. If I could have pressed "rewind" to six weeks before this happened, the universe seemed to be sending all the go signs I needed. I felt momentum from publishing my first freelance articles with the *Washington Post* and *Parents* magazine. And the start of summer always fueled my creative energy. I was excited to gain a little more space in the mornings for sleep once school ended for both kids, yet as quickly as the space came between the unplanned pause in childcare and broken appliances, it closed again. I got busier and didn't carve out the self-care or creative time I desperately needed.

I am blessed to have a nanny; I know being able to make that investment in my career comes with financial privilege and I was intentional about this when choosing among our childcare options. But I'll admit at times, having to earn enough money to afford an in-home caregiver felt like another double-edged sword. But if you've ever experienced financial instability, especially in your childhood, you already know that you'll push yourself in sometimes wild directions to outwit the odds. Many of us also shape our whole lives around the fear of not having enough money. I chose my career in business very carefully, despite my early love of dance, writing, and music, because I was driven to have enough income to someday have freedom not just over how I managed my work but also over my time.

Of course, young me made some assumptions that didn't quite pan out. But I'm not going to sugarcoat this. If you are trying to climb over or tunnel under the wealth gap, you already know it contributes to an extra helping of mental load, decision fatigue, and chronic stress. You can also get tripped up by scarcity thinking. Changing the trajectory for ourselves and generational outcomes for our kids usually means pushing way beyond what's comfortable. So, just know that I know how big of a deal it is to squeeze yourself into spaces that weren't designed for you. Especially when it's to make a living for the life you know in your soul you and your family deserve.

So, cognitive (aka mental load) is one thing, but I didn't learn about the second ghost, decision fatigue, which is something else entirely, until I stumbled across it in my research. These choices we make throughout the day, big and small decisions like managing uneven childcare, not only carve our attention into little pieces but also hold biological weight, as in the number of decisions we can make each day has a limit. And that weight can also lead to guess what? Yep, more stress and mental fog. Okay, so I realize you probably know what the mental load is, but we're going to do a little mini-refresher with some of the lesser-known perils and strategies to reduce it.

Meet Ghost Number Two: Mental (Cognitive) Load

If you've ever read the Charles Dickens classic "A Christmas Carol" you may remember that the main character, Ebenezer Scrooge, was haunted by three different ghosts. Each one was a little scarier than the last, and cumulatively enough to take even that grouchy, self-confident character apart. Well, we have our own ghosts because they're invisible when you first encounter them. But in time, they become scarier and all together, if unchecked, they will create a special kind of hell inside of your otherwise beautiful life.

So, before having kids, it's unusual to learn about the mental load or how it works exactly. I'm sure you know about it now if you've been a mom for more than a minute but you probably haven't received enough detail about how it works, or the other top stressors that come right along with it, like scarcity thinking, the impact of time scarcity on your mental bandwidth and decision fatigue, to reduce their impact.

Cognitive load isn't new, you've certainly experienced it before. But once you take on parenting, with the other things you usually do, without any adjustments to your support infrastructure, processes, or self-care practices, this seemingly small thing can become *the thing* to push you over the emotional, or professional, cliff.

It Turns Out, Our Brains Have Limits

Although you've probably heard about "the mental load" of motherhood, cognitive load is not just a parenting phenomenon. It hits moms, who are more likely to manage the household, kids, and paid work in parallel, particularly hard. One of the first Mom's Hierarchy of Needs research studies, in 2017, was about the effects of cognitive load on everything from work, career trajectory, wellness, and relationships to parenting. Interestingly, no matter how much help moms in the study had or didn't have, their financial situation, type of careers they had or if they didn't work for pay at all, 98% of those surveyed found the mental load the most persistent source of stress contributing to feeling overwhelmed.

Most of us contend with the mental load and its impact daily. One evening I rushed home from the office and flew through the door. As usual, I was in a panic about relieving our nanny on time. But I was late anyway. This was almost five years ago, and my commute from that job was always complicated by reliance on the trains and random late-day meetings when it looked better to be there in person. Now, not everyone that I worked with was there in person; many were remote. But if the meeting involved Boston-based people, my then boss wanted me to show my face. And I liked getting to know people. But if the meeting started late, as they often did, they would end late, too. And it felt sticky leaving a meeting early to pick up my kids, since I was usually the only one who needed to do so. Although most of my colleagues were parents, they were overwhelmingly men, whose partners handled pickup and empty nesters, free from managing their days around childcare and school schedules. They also had more tenure in the company than I did. In hindsight, I did some pretty ridiculous things to be there in person even when it didn't make sense. Like trying to fit two or three round-trip commutes into a single day, because I needed to be "seen" at the office. Even if I wanted to just do a late-day meeting remotely, I would need to leave the office when there was a meeting-free window to commute home. But this often wasn't possible so I'd join calls from the noisy and crowded trains.

That day, I almost jogged that last block and was thrilled when I finally made it home. I gave quick hugs to the kids, who were four and eight at the time, and started to cook. I've internalized certain deadlines, like when dinner happens, to stay on schedule with bedtime. Which, of course, influences how well things go that evening and the next morning. While I was waiting for the chicken to brown, I wanted to see if anything time sensitive came up in that last meeting. As I scanned the flurry of work emails on my phone, I could hear my kids arguing about something in my son's bedroom. I couldn't see them from the kitchen, but I could hear it escalating. And since my husband wasn't home, I stepped out of the kitchen to figure out what was going on. "Mom, she's trying to take my Legos," my son said angrily. I saw the Lego clutched tightly in my daughter's hand. She responded, matter-of-factly for a four-year old, "this one is mine." I held her hand and said, "Honey, you have so many Legos. Why take your brother's? Please come into the kitchen, where I can . . ." I was already irritated by my children fussing and suddenly, the fire alarm went off. Very, very loudly. Although I thought I lowered the temperature for the chicken, I had left it on high heat so it started to burn. I forgot that I was cooking because I was already thinking about five other things. There was that email check, worrying about remembering to pay my nanny extra for that day since I was late. I was also mentally rehashing the meeting. When the kids started arguing, that interruption managed to take the part of my brain that was working on dinner, offline. My neighbors started texting and calling shortly after. So, I had to turn off the stove and open several windows to clear the smoke. As I frantically wished for the alarm—which, by then triggered all of the building alarms to go off—to stop, I was lucky that our downstairs neighbor came up to help. But the whole thing was noisy, embarrassing, and, of course, time-consuming.

How often have you berated yourself for not being "on top of things"? Right, probably too many times to count, but if you revisit these memories with an understanding of the mental load, you free yourself. Not only to see the circumstances differently but to preempt them to a greater degree.

That Includes Your Working Memory

Think about your working memory as a bookshelf that has room for no more than seven books. That's right I'm going to repeat that because no one likes to hear this part. Not 70 or 17 but 7. As we constantly navigate our to-do lists, the act of letting something slip off that mental bookshelf is something our brains just don't like. For example, have you ever woken up in the middle of the night, unable to sleep because you thought about something you needed to do? Like an email you forgot to send or a birthday party that needs to be planned? Whatever it was doesn't matter. What mattered is that you thought about it at 2 a.m. And because your brain doesn't want to let it slip off the working memory bookshelf, your brain tries mightily to "hold onto" that action item, and keeps you awake.

When I interviewed Dr. April Seifert, psychologist, researcher, and CEO of Sprocket CX for Mom's Hierarchy of Needs she said, "What everyone calls *mom brain*, really is the mental load. Any time we've got way too much on our minds that we're trying not to forget, we experience cognitive load."[3] She conducted experimental research during her graduate school career and had to be able to "turn off people's ability to reason and think deliberately" in order to study the phenomenon they were interested in. She said, "The way we turned off their higher-order cognition is to put them under something called *cognitive load*. We gave them all of these really complicated math problems or asked them to remember 9- or 10-digit numbers and then sent them to class. Pretty quickly the other professors asked us to stop because people couldn't get any meaningful work done after this experiment."

So, absorb that for a moment. Basically, we're doing a version of this to ourselves—overloading our cognitive capacity—everyday while trying to manage careers, family, and other commitments. And we're still drowning in post-pandemic changes to our economy, health, and communities. A lot of things we're dealing with are new. So, processing changes to established routines takes more brain space. Especially when the new routines replace activities we used to internalize or store in our long-term memory. For example, if you went from driving to work daily to remote work and then commuting on a hybrid schedule, that's a lot of routine shifts. Or for those of you who always work on-site, you've likely had to react to new safety protocols, industry conditions, and revisions to your work processes. Some of you changed jobs, lines of work, or paused paid work altogether during the "Great Resignation" of 2021. Your life is different in some meaningful way based on what happened and there's a good chance your brain is still trying to catch up.

Meet Ghost Number Three: Decision Fatigue

As I coaxed the oatmeal to a slow simmer, I thought about how quiet it was until my little one appeared with a loud "boo" followed by her stealth smile. Nothing is quite as fun for her as jump-scaring mommy. Pumpkin scones were baking for their snacks, but in my multitasking haze, I forgot to set the timer. So, I looked through the oven window, trying to guesstimate how far along they were, every few minutes. Earlier, I woke up uneasily from a series of anxiety dreams, mostly about how to schedule today's back-up care sitter. Should I take my son to soccer by myself or walk him to school to go with the coach? And since my husband won't be home tonight, should I keep my daughter in her pajamas post-bath or like last time, will she want to play in the dirt while we wait? Yes, this really happened the week before and I had to bathe her all over again. It seems like I'm focused on minutia, but these details often mean the difference between everyone getting to sleep on time or not, including me. And being somewhat rested for another day of full-on sprints. School. Soccer practice. Meetings at work. Dinner. Post dinner. So, the bedtime ritual always comingles with the other deadlines. I know you know.

Thankfully, my nanny's husband's surgery was successful and the next month she was back. I didn't know then that she would have a different health issue of her own, which would prompt her to quit and require me to find someone new. And start the intense search for care all over again about two years later. Of course, that happened during another fragile juncture in my career. You may be wondering how much about my work fragility was a coincidence and how much was causal from all of the stress and mental load I was under. Well, spending a good amount of mental energy fretting about childcare, or eldercare (which I'll touch on later because my sister and I share responsibilities for our parents and have for a long time), is huge. But the unwritten rule of modern work and senior roles is to be "always available," which doesn't work for most parents and certainly not for most moms. Also, anything that competes for your brain space threatens your health. And anything that threatens your health threatens your professional and personal growth. Women, as I shared previously, have more to do in most families and receive less grace in the workplace.

How has your career changed after kids? Is it just how you feel about your relationship with work or has your growth trajectory shifted? Again, we lament every miscalculation in our professional lives and view the missteps as strictly personal failures. There's a big picture for you at any given time: the current state of the world, the support systems you have in and outside of the workplace, plus the stress that you carry. There are options to navigate these very real dynamics but first you have to acknowledge that they are there.

How Mental Load Contributes to Decision Fatigue and the Influence of Time Scarcity

Before all of this brings you too far into a depression, remember that moms are multitasking, time-bending, miracle workers. And we make extraordinary contributions, not just in the lives of our kids and family members but also in every field and community. We are super capable. But we pay a toll for wrestling that to-do list in our brains. And it's not just the discomfort from being nibbled by 1,000 little decisions, but as I shared previously, the health cost is real. Remember when I mentioned how your working memory battles mightily to track the list of things you don't want to forget? The trade-offs associated with prioritizing what to do within the limited time you really have (versus the unlimited time you imagined you'd have) creates a downward spiral of weighing trade-offs. Should I start laundry? It's too late . . . well, maybe I start the load tonight and finish in the morning. What about email, I never did get back to so and so. Okay, let me get to that email before I go to bed. Oh no, the discounted registration window for camp is closing. Okay, maybe that's what I'll do as soon as they're asleep. And on it goes until . . . *beep* . . . that unexpected call or text message comes in to completely change everything.

I love this quote from a piece in the *New York Times*[4] about decision fatigue. "Decision fatigue helps explain why ordinarily sensible people get angry at colleagues and families, splurge on clothes, buy junk food at the supermarket and can't resist the dealer's offer to rustproof their new car. No matter how rational and high-minded you try to be, you can't make decision after decision without paying a biological price. It's different from ordinary physical fatigue—you're not consciously aware of being tired—but you're low on mental energy. The more choices you make throughout the day, the harder each one becomes for your brain, and eventually it looks for shortcuts." Which is often either to make a rash, out-of-character decision or to make no decision at all. Sound familiar?

Decision fatigue and strategies to reduce it have been getting more attention as another "neuroscience-y" way to enhance productivity and career efficacy and an indicator of something that undermines our mental health. So, as you may remember, the late Steve Jobs, the founder and CEO of Apple, was famous for his uniform of black turtlenecks and jeans. It's because he didn't want to waste his brain space matching or picking out his clothes each day. Of course, a mom would probably get a lot of side-eye for something like that. But there are other people who decide to eat the same thing every day for lunch or breakfast. I totally do this now by the way and I'll share more on this later in my favorite systems section on food, which you can access in the Afterword. Or the routine meal prep and planning (yes, I do that, too) for this reason.

There are many options to better manage our limited capacity for decision-making. Again the need to make as many decisions as we do is only amplified by the disproportionate time-scarcity hit most moms absorb. The third ghost, the impact of scarcity, is no joke.

But remember, seeing the ghosts creates options. When they're no longer invisible drains on your mental energy, you get to choose your own adventure. You may really enjoy picking out specific outfits for your kids, or meals for your family, or weighing the hundreds of cereal choices in the grocery store.

And if you love getting into the details of that, awesome! Keep that on your priority list. It's all about knowing what is meaningful and important to you, and how to change your approach and reduce the mental health toll for anything that isn't.

And How Some of Us Also Face Weathering

I was at an event last year when I heard the term *weathering* about mothers in the Black community for the first time during a keynote presentation by Dr. Michael Curry.[5] Although at that point, I had read quite a bit of research about underlying causes in the Black maternal health crisis, which as you may know just about doubles the risk of morbidity, death for a mom, or her baby, for Black moms in America. So, I was mesmerized by data about the cumulative impact of facing structural barriers, a mix of racism and sexism and how that disproportionately affects Black women. As stated in an article published by Harvard's School of Public Health,[6] Arline Geronimus said, "While most women in their 20s and early 30s are considered low-risk, black women may be weathered and biologically older than their chronological age, which makes them more subject to health complications at younger ages. This is true even among highly educated or professional women, such as Serena Williams or Shalon Irving." Also in the article, she adds, "The U.S. lacks policies that support women who want both careers and parenthood, a gap that can lead professional women to postpone childbearing until their late 30s or 40s. . . . . As a group, black mothers in their mid- to late 30s have five times the maternal mortality rate of black teen mothers, although the older mothers generally have greater educational or economic resources and access to health care."

I'm very, very lucky to have my mother but her health is not what it would've been without the cumulative erosion from her life experiences. When I flash back to childhood memories of her, she was so patient, energetic, calm, and joyful. She was just happy to be alive, and in the 20 years that followed, she dealt with a lot of adversity. She was always such a house person, tending to our yard and gardens with such love, that I don't think she ever fully recovered from the grief of losing our home. There were so many financial issues that suddenly altered her daily life. And managing the constant stress of debt collectors calling, asking friends and family for money, ultimately taking three different jobs, including cleaning and babysitting, to pay our bills reduced her. She became a different person under relentless pressure. So, now in her older age, the long-term toll on her health is visible.

In effect, being battered by too many environmental stressors prematurely ages us. Yes, you saw that right. And it's playing a hidden role in the health of millions of people. Black women are weathering even when they have economic and environmental advantages. Weathering also affects people living in poverty or otherwise underserved communities, regardless of their race, gender, or ethnicity.

Most moms carry an unruly amount of stress. And in communities of color, there is an extra helping that comes from the weight of navigating systems that weren't designed for us. We have to push extra hard, which takes a lot of mental and physical energy that ultimately shapes us into different people. Usually, we're a little less sensitive to repeated stressors and become a bit edgier and more guarded. So, whether you are "weathered" or not, a mom of color or not, or feeling the weight of being in other historically overlooked groups, like those with disabilities or LGBTQ+, if you find yourself starting to feel detached, or minimizing your or your family's needs in ways that feel concerning, seek out help. And lean into mental health and care systems that are available to you. And, yes, that might mean talking to your primary care doctor about options, calling a crisis help line or your employer's employee assistance plan if you or your partner have those benefits for immediate support. If it's less time sensitive, find a therapist or another form of support for your mental and emotional health, like a group program. Seriously, if you feel like you are in peril, don't wait. There's no amount of meditation or deep breathing that will help an acute mental health crisis. And keep your eyes on the prize: ultimately, we want to stop the cycle of self-sacrifice or weathering for our own daughters, many of whom will become mothers someday, and you also want to have the beautiful bright life you deserve.

Okay, so, back to weathering. I'm going to encourage everyone of you whether you are part of the Black community or not to get really proactive about your preventative health care. And that includes not only the self-care that you do at home like exercise, deep breathing, time with friends, or proper nutrition but making sure you attend every one of those recommended screenings based on your stage of life and personal health history. Because weathering isn't the only stress phenomenon at play here. Years of overworking can also manifest into high blood pressure, heart disease, and all types of very real, very scary, yet often very avoidable, physical conditions.

Women, in part because of caregiving[7] and also due to biology, are at greater risk for stress-related everything, for example, autoimmune diseases,[8] fatal heart disease,[9] and after menopause high blood pressure,[10] among others. But then there are extra factors. For example, Black, Indigenous, and people of color moms are at even greater risk for certain conditions, and they may differ based on your race, ethnicity, or culture. So, again my point here is to be vigilant about your medical care, not just your preventative self-care. And when we get into methods, in Section Three, I'll do a much deeper dive on how to systematize in a way that works for your schedule and makes it easier to keep up with these things.

Notes

1. https://bipartisanpolicy.org/blog/bpc-morning-consult-pregnancy-discrimination/
2. https://health.clevelandclinic.org/scarcity-mindset
3. https://en.wikipedia.org/wiki/Cognitive_load
4. https://www.nytimes.com/2011/08/21/magazine/do-you-suffer-from-decision-fatigue.html
5. https://www.linkedin.com/in/michael-curry-esq-6761777/
6. https://hsph.harvard.edu/news/america-is-failing-its-black-mothers/
7. https://www.apa.org/pi/about/publications/caregivers/faq/health-effects
8. https://med.stanford.edu/news/all-news/2024/02/women-autoimmune.html
9. https://www.heart.org/en/news/2024/02/09/the-slowly-evolving-truth-about-heart-disease-and-women
10. https://www.mayoclinic.org/diseases-conditions/high-blood-pressure/symptoms-causes/syc-20373410

Chapter 3

Emerge from the (Mental) Fog

So, you may be wondering: where do I start? First, you're already much further than you were. Understanding the key concepts makes it a lot easier to adapt strategies that work in your life, and maintain the will to do so, even when going through the inevitable trial and error.

This chapter aims to focus on some key components of the tool kit you can use and adapt to reduce mental load, decision fatigue, and the impact of time scarcity, which is yet another natural by-product of living with time famine, also known as *time poverty*, and not having enough time to do what you need to do. As I've tried to explain unlike some of our other challenges, each of the three connect. After all, if you're not dealing with time scarcity, you're less likely to be consistently managing decision fatigue. The mental load can be a by-product of time famine, too. They interrelate as do the solutions. It took years of research, hearing from thousands of moms in my studies, and having over 100 conversations with doctors, mental health experts, and other researchers—not to mention the many amazing books I've read—to come up with the mom-friendly versions of these widely accepted best practices to improve our well-being. Just know, nothing has to be perfect for it to be effective. Remember, you are doing incredible and important work every day in a society that wasn't set up to support you. We are in the land of creative adaptation right now. You will soon find yourself noticing more often the schedule collisions and opportunities to assert your preferences on your calendar, with your loved ones and, most important, with yourself.

The Best Way to Reduce Cognitive (Over)Load or Decision Fatigue Means Doing Less

I know, I know. The last thing you want to hear is that you should shorten your to-do list. Nobody likes to hear this. I certainly didn't. But it is reality. And I realize you're probably busier than you ever were, so the idea of cutting things might feel impossible. And there are seasons of life where you're dealing with a crisis that demands much more from you. But don't rush to think about the how yet—because we'll get into that as this book progresses. For now, let's review these principles because some version of this can help alleviate stress. I recommend a combination of approaches based on what really works for your life, season, and circumstances: outsourcing, spouse sourcing (if you are partnered), and eliminating things altogether. This often means setting boundaries, which we will also cover in more depth in Chapter 5, because I know boundaries don't always work for us, especially in the workplace.

Create Flexible Rules for Repeated (aka Boring) Obligations

Nope, that does not include other people's shoulds, nor does it mean throwing yourself in front of the productivity train. Once you have a clear sense of what your real priorities are, not other people's expectations but what feels aligned with your values, gifts, desired commitments, and ambitions for this stage of your life, then eliminating unnecessary activities is the next step to get efficient with what you care most about, right now.

For example, do you respond to every birthday party invitation, buy the gifts, and do the commuting to and from for every classmate your child or children have? Think about it: do they need to go to every single one? And if so, do you need to be the one to manage that whole process, especially if you live in a two-adult household? Right. Unless it really feels values aligned and important to you to make sure your child is faithful to the birthday party circuit, trim some of those commitments. Some moms I meet only choose to attend birthday parties for close friends or when it's convenient to travel to. Otherwise, they politely decline all of them. Some parents always bring gift certificates versus trying to pick out the perfect gift. At times, I've shipped a gift ahead of or even after the party to avoid another stop at a local store and time spent picking, choosing, and then waiting in line. But to help reduce the mental energy spent on that particular task, within an age range—for example, kids under age 10—I'll buy books. If they're over age 10, and are more likely to have strong preferences about what they'll read or a broader library that I might overlap with, then I pick something broadly "creative," whether that's Lego sets or art-making tools or kits.

Batch, boring repeated but necessary tasks you can't outsource or spouse source but you can do a larger amount less frequently. For example, this can include activities like bill paying once per month versus every time a new one comes in, checking emails or social media inboxes every few hours instead of all day long, folding laundry weekly, or making school snacks or bread every few weeks for that matter. Yes, you can batch make just about anything. So, when I recently stayed with my fabulous cousin and her family, we had a brief discussion about pancakes. She suggested we have pancakes in the morning.

I asked if she had buttermilk, and she looked at me as if I had four heads. Later, when we had a brief debate about the fact that she uses a mix and I do not, she nicknamed me "Pioneer Woman" for several hours. Family can do this sort of thing, be really really honest with you but in a funny and nonthreatening way. If, like me, you're interested in from scratch meals, there are so many ways to be efficient with that by batching. But, cooking like that also takes extra time, so it's not necessary. It's a fun, meaningful necessity-dressed-like-a-hobby as far as I'm concerned. But if it interests you, I'm happy to share more on that in the systems guides mentioned in the Afterword.

So, it's not only cooking, which is a pretty common example. There are many things that require some mental bandwidth and you can still make progress working in power batches of 20 to 30 minutes, versus needing hours of time. So, I hold some calendar blocks for these activities. If not, the type of "exploding-undone-task" just creates a lot more stress and often cost. But if it's scheduled in manageable chunks for when you have childcare (and if needed, eldercare) or when your children are otherwise occupied or can participate, it helps.

Keep Doing Less, Intentionally, for Routine Outsourceable Tasks

The goal here is to both eliminate to-dos altogether and streamline how your desired priorities are done, when that's possible. Now of course, outsource and spouse source as much as you possibly can so there's less and less for you to do all the time. Really. Because as you're taking on more cognitive complexity and more logistical management all the time, as the kids get older, the complexity only increases. It's one thing to get a baby to sleep, but it's an entirely different type of thing to try to explain love, discretion, war, character development, or the Internal Revenue Service to your middle schooler. My point is, you are going to keep getting busier, so *do not* think you will be less busy as your child(ren) age. People might try to tell you that, but it is just not true.

Plus, you want to do more for yourself and replace the never-done tasks that aren't that vital to anyone with fueling activities, healing activities, and learning activities—those moves that help you to grow and become healthier and happier, especially with activities that are not either within what Dr. Gaye Hendricks calls, "your zone of genius"[1] or tied directly to your goals. For example, do you need to drive your kids to every appointment or soccer practice? Do you need to order more toilet paper, or can your partner or do it. If not, do you have a household cleaner or caregiver who can add this to their list? If not, can you subscribe to it in some way from a local or national retailer, so it's automated. Yes, try to get rid of these boring tasks, but if you can't, batch them so they're happening on a routine and not consuming your mental space at the wrong times.

Don't Include Repeated Points of Friction or Effort in Your Professional Life

Okay, work can be much harder, so take a look there, too. If you're responsible for a monthly operating report and find that, inevitably, you are trying to finish it late on Sunday nights, every single time, that's a task that is ready for some reinvention. Of course, I know there are real landmines for women for setting boundaries and stepping outside of the lines of what's expected, especially at work. And we will dive deeper into boundaries in Chapter 6 and how to tap into your inner reservoir of courage, calm, and creativity. But consider whether the process to get the information for that report is working, or do you need lots of other people or data from lots of sources? Can you just delegate the gathering of the input to someone else, on your team, another team, or someone in a supportive role? Can you push back on the size of the report successfully or perhaps its frequency? Can you create a standard summary that you just copy and paste into every report instead of crafting a custom introduction or email? Trim, trim, trim, wherever and whatever you can! But start with things that tend to frustrate you or where you feel like you're stuck in the same dilemma over and over.

Strategically Use Rituals to Reduce the Overload

Have you ever read a productivity book? You'll likely see the recommendation to "use willpower" to "build habits," rituals, or routines into your schedule. I think I've read all of them. And these books are mostly written by men, and rarely written with parents, caregivers, or moms in mind, which makes some of the assumptions they make about how much "control" we have over our schedules laughable. You may be anti-schedule somewhere in your soul. And there was a part of me that resisted being on another schedule even for myself for a long time because I was drowning in the work of keeping on top of schedules in my professional life, for the kids, my partner, and my parents. But, once I learned more about the neuroscience behind stress and performance, I had to admit there are many good reasons for this advice. And it can be adapted in ways that really work for mom-life.

Remember how your working memory has a pretty tight limit on what fits? One of the greatest "productivity tools" is to have your brain work for you versus against you. And to put as many things as possible into your long-term storage where it's not competing for space in your working memory. That's why almost any productivity book you read will recommend creating habits and routines. Even though you probably learned important life skills like driving a car or brushing your teeth many years ago you probably don't think about the immense amount of complexity associated with those tasks when you do them. Why? Basically, they are so ritualized that you are not relying on your working or short-term memory. They are part of your long-term memory so those tasks feel effortless and almost ingrained.

Depending on the age, health, and independence of your kids, creating room on the calendar for a habit can be incredibly difficult because caregiving tends to be highly unpredictable, whether it's for babies, kids, teens, or for your parents or other adults. Basically, for anyone. And if you're lucky to have healthy kids who follow expected trajectories and milestones, it's still very uneven.

Caring for adults, especially if these adults are aging parents or have complex medical needs, is also extremely dynamic. What is predictable in most families, however, is that due to the stubborn age-old gendered divide[2] most of the housework, childcare,[3] and cognitive load to plan it all[4] falls to moms when they are partnered with dads. Moms who are single, depending on the age, health, and independence of their kids, often don't have any backup to step away. They tend to, as most of us do, rely solely on whatever primary childcare they have for paid work. That is, if they're fortunate to have a primary childcare set up at all. Later, in Chapter 7 I'll do a deeper dive on how to strategically use (and think about) nontraditional or even hidden childcare options based on your circumstances and needs.

Here are a few ideas of rituals that may feel supportive:

- **Keep a journal or notebook next to your bed.** I know you've heard this one before, but it really works well for me and could work for you, too. Experiment with it. I take 5 or 10 minutes most nights to do a mini "brain dump" on paper of uncaptured to-dos and priorities for the next day. Whatever that is for you, just get it out on paper (or video or a notes app). And you will be surprised at how it improves your sleep. I write down the three priorities I want to focus on for the next day, sometimes along with two or three other tasks that are less time sensitive.

- **Julia Cameron's "morning pages" offers sage creativity advice from her book.** *The Artists Way* to journal write for three, full-sized pages long hand (not typed) about anything that may be on your mind every morning. This one is tougher to do with kids because well, mornings. Although I love it, I don't do it every day faithfully. But I am pretty good about doing it on the weekends, when I travel or on school vacation days when I have more time in the mornings. But I imagine it would still be powerful as nighttime practice, although please note in the book she is emphatic about the morning slot. Her practice is centered on creativity through a very spiritual lens, which isn't going to resonate with everyone. Her process also involves carving out a *lot* of self-care time, which is a beautiful thing, but the way she advocates for it, and the amount of it, just may not work for every mom out there.
- **Process difficult situations with a three-part series of quick journaling sessions.** Many years ago, before having kids, I took a cognitive restructuring course at the Massachusetts General Brigham Hospital's Benson Henry Institute, where they shared results from a study by Dr. James Pennebaker of the University of Texas at Austin about a unique journaling technique. There have been hundreds of other studies since then, but it was basically designed to address processing past traumas or difficult experiences. The rules for us were to set a timer for 20 minutes and write whatever we wanted about that difficult experience in a journal. And to repeat this exercise for three days in a row to release the experience. I have used this same exercise, over the years, many times to navigate something difficult from the safety of the page. You may not need this if you have a therapist, peer group, or regular space to share difficulties or traumas. But, wow, I love being able to not dress up my feelings and let all of the venom out where no one will read it.

What all of these techniques have in common, whether it's the expressive writing techniques for creativity, mental health, or capturing your to-do list for productivity, is taking what's floating around in your brain and putting it somewhere to free yourself from the stress of ruminating on it or trying to remember it.

See (Some Amount of) Structure as Your Friend

When I interviewed psychiatrist and trauma specialist Dr. Nichole C. Brathwaite, MD, early in the pandemic she explained that structure is our friend and helps stabilize many people who are prone to anxiety or depression. The routines of things like getting up at a certain time, preparing or consuming breakfast in a certain way, navigating drop-off and/or pickup, having a schedule in your paid work, creating routines for your unpaid work, ritualizing some partner time if you are partnered, taking space for reflection, worship (if you are a person of faith), friends, and/or community engagement all helps you drop anchor into the rhythm of life. But remember you get to choose what time is used for your daily anchors; they don't have to look like someone else's. But even if you're not prone to anxiety or depression, caregiving is intense and can strain your resilience muscles, not to mention your patience and presence. Structure can help bookend your days and protect time for what you value. And when you are a caregiver and also employee or business owner, unstructured days usually don't.

Begin to build a new schedule that ideally incorporates frequent breaks for your health, deep work, creative pursuits, and family. We're talking about daily self-care here! I will spend more time on exactly how to do this throughout Section Two in the ways we need as moms, when we get into systems we can tailor for the top of the Mom's Hierarchy of Needs activities, and throughout Section Three, including where to find sources of support.

Stay in Flow (Whenever Possible) for Important Deep Work or for Self-Care

Another real game changer for me was to understand the concept of flow, originally described by Mihály Csíkszentmihályi[5] in his book, *Finding Flow: the Psychology of Engagement with Everyday Life*.[6] Even if you haven't taken the time to study flow in detail you've probably experienced it. It's usually when you're doing something that you love or that you're interested in and feel like you're in a mode when time freezes because you're enjoying the activity so much. You're deeply focused and you're able to get through the task in record time or with record efficiency. Oh . . . and you're probably not being interrupted either. Right? That is an important part of being in flow and staying there, which is incredibly hard to do when our devices, kids, and colleagues can track us everywhere. Double that if you have those kids at home and don't have childcare. Most experts will recommend a 90-minute to two-hour window for a flow state. Without going into the details, know that most experts agree your brain gets tired and wants to do something else after about 90 minutes or two hours at most. So, if you find yourself reading that paragraph for the tenth time or wanting to scroll social media instead of finishing your presentation, that's a good sign that you have hit a limit and you are best served to get up take a walk, have some water, do a quick meditation, dance, sleep, or rest. Remember rest? Basically, do whatever it is that will refresh you before returning to that task or something else.

How to Put This All Together

You may be rolling out of your chair, imagining what it would take to optimize your schedule and your routine so that you have at least one 90-minute uninterrupted block each day. Having that time to focus on your highest priority work or self-care activities is the ideal, but I realize it doesn't often work in beyond-busy mom life as often as we might like. If ever. So, I had to work up to this for a deep work block and still, there are days and weeks that everything goes in a different direction, and I just can't make it happen. Somedays I enjoy a full hour of movement and time to myself in the morning, after I drop off the kids. But other days it's 15 minutes, like when my kids have super early sports activities. And there are times I choose to do something that is beneficial to me in another way, like attend a conference or travel to a special event, which means there is no deep work or long self-care block that day.

You may be thinking, "wait, Leslie, when am I possibly going to do these things?" Don't worry, we'll get more into the practical realities, including the scheduling part, in the remaining sections of the book. We started with mindset first because understanding why this is important is key to recognizing the little ways you can intervene for yourself. So, starting with the fundamentals and freeing your mind to think about your circumstances and opportunities differently sets you up for success.

It's taken me *years* to research, understand, and then successfully do this. I'm explaining this step by step in the order that I believe is the most helpful. So, after learning how to free your mind in this section, Section Two is all about easing the workload before we really talk about getting a grasp on your fuel sources to ramp up your energy (spoiler alert, with better health) in Section Three. With context, you can do anything, including committing to build on these things in your own beautiful way and develop systems you really love. Most important, you will most likely do this in a fraction of the time that it took for me, which is my fervent wish for you.

Notes

1. https://hendricks.com/gay-talks-about-taking-the-big-leap-into-the-genius-zone-on-the-inspired-money-podcast-with-andy-wang/

2. https://www.sciencedirect.com/science/article/abs/pii/S0927537120300257
3. https://www.pewresearch.org/social-trends/2023/01/24/gender-and-parenting/
4. https://onlinelibrary.wiley.com/doi/10.1111/jomf.13057
5. https://www.goodreads.com/author/show/27446.Mih_ly_Cs_kszentmih_lyi
6. https://www.goodreads.com/en/book/show/66321

Section Two

EASE YOUR WORKLOAD

Chapter 4

Shift, Trim, Eliminate, and Repeat

"Laura, it's so great to see you!" I gave a warm hug to a friend whom I hadn't seen in quite a while. At the time, she was in the midst of a career transition so we met up at one of my favorite local bakeries, Flour, in the South End of Boston, to discuss her interests and explore introductions I could make. As we chatted about her search, our kids, and life in general, I enjoyed a dreamy raspberry lemon cake, with a light buttercream frosting. It's the kind of dessert that I used to make regularly, especially in my post-culinary school years. But now, I rarely invest time in fun, yet labor-intensive baking projects. My baking has moved from gateau opera and hazelnut tarts to batch freezing brioche, chocolate banana bread, and pumpkin scones for the kids. As we wrapped up our patio conversation, and went to take our dishes inside, I threw away a napkin in the outdoor trash can, but the wind took it and smeared buttercream along the edge of the bin. When Laura came outside, she asked, "Leslie, are you cleaning the garbage can?" I looked up, napkins in hand as I tried to scrub the excess buttercream from the side. I realized, how silly it was for me to feel the need to clean an outdoor trash can in a public place. I confessed, "Why, yes, I think you now know everything you need to know about why I'm so overloaded."

Even if it's not cleaning public trash cans, are you holding onto some "should" that doesn't really serve you? There are some activities you probably feel compelled to do, that are almost automatic in nature, like a reflex. You might find yourself cleaning counters, picking up Legos, responding to that "reply all" email chain that doesn't require a response, or running around frantically trying to preclean your home, before your paid house cleaner comes. I'm still prone to self-sabotage, but I've become savvier and more intentional about disrupting my go-to patterns of overdo.

To consistently decrease your time spent on never-done tasks and increase your mental and physical energy, you need to ease your workload. There's no way around that. Some of that can be done with trimming and cutting things that matter to you less right now, and we'll spend time on exactly that. But I want to be clear, it also involves getting more support. It's really a both/and situation. Remember those stats I shared in Chapter 1 about the plight of mothers? And how the US Surgeon General declared "parent stress" a public health crisis? Well, this is about your health! This is about optimizing your chances to have as many joyful, healthy years as possible. So, during this process and yes, I realize it is a process, please keep your eyes on the prize. Change can be complicated, and it will not feel natural to make these changes, because again, we are discouraged from doing things to care for ourselves, and we are celebrated when we serve others. But it is essential to override this programming. And the endgame—access to your own health and well-being, your birthright—is worth it.

Yes, I want you to get that promotion, build that empire or lifesaving nonprofit you've been thinking about. I'd love for you to have the accolades, resources, and fulfillment you richly deserve. But if your health is undermined because of the conditions most of us operate in, then you will not achieve the same things that you really want to achieve with the necessary fuel. Your health is what matters here, and all of your other goals and needs will follow from that. And just in case you need further convincing, it's not only great for you and your career but also for your family. Countless studies validate what many of us feel. If we aren't doing well mentally or emotionally, it can be extremely harmful to our kids in the short and long term. The stress hormone cortisol, which left unchecked can lead to chronic illnesses, has been shown to be elevated in children[1] when it's elevated in parents. Now, when I learned this, of course I had an internal Type A tantrum because it felt like yet another parenting mistake I was making. But we can't control everything and my point here is not to add guilt. Nobody needs that. Know that as parents we adapt and grow all of the time. What's important is to note that caring for yourself is another way to care for your kids.

Remember the ghost of scarcity thinking? Well, again, in the beautifully researched book Scarcity,[2] Authors Sendhil Mullainathan and Eldar Shafir share multiple examples of how differently we do things when we have extra slack versus when our time, money, food, or other resources are limited. In the book, they describe packing for a trip as an example to illustrate how scarcity reshapes our behavior. You know how you make fewer trade-offs if you have a large suitcase for a short trip versus a small one? For example, you might put in those fabulous sandals you rarely wear, or bring your favorite moisturizers. But if you're packing for that same trip with a small suitcase, you're forced to make different trade-offs. You can't possibly pack the same clothes, shoes, bags, or skincare you might otherwise consider. And, of course, traveling with kids is an entirely different packing challenge altogether. We do the same thing, with our time, all of the time. And we're often so stretched that we try to shrink things down to their smallest possible size, with the hope that everything will fit in the metaphorical suitcase. But shrinking, or stuffing our responsibilities into too little space, is often to our own detriment. In the book the authors explain that "having 'slack' allows us the feeling of abundance. Slack is not just an efficiency, it's a mental luxury. Abundance does not just allow us to buy more goods, it affords us the luxury of packing poorly, the luxury of not having to think, as well as the luxury of not minding mistakes."

Do you remember what it feels like to have that type of time luxury? Maybe it was on a business trip when you traveled solo, or perhaps it was pre-kids. But for most moms, time to think or make mistakes without repercussions or self-recrimination is rare. Of course, for those who battle against other forms of scarcity in parallel, like lack of money, physical safety, food, *and* a lack of time, it's a different game. That isn't the focus of this book, because there are different needs, strategies, and levers to pull for those living on the socioeconomic margins. However, it's important to note that as we move through life, and observe those around us, scarcity tightens not only opportunities but creates extra cognitive complexity and exhaustion for those who suffer from it.

Strategic Trimming

We're like Olympic swimmers, trying to shave a few seconds from our time each day. Some of us trim every interaction by spending less time with friends, family members, and colleagues, whereas others shrink down the time spent on household basics, like meal prep and cooking with simpler or prepared alternatives. Others still shrink their workloads in their paid jobs or choose careers with shorter or more predictable schedules. And some of us (okay me) try to shrink just about everything all at once. However, there are risks in that. Being too efficient can feel like a hollow victory. Life's moments can begin to feel like the essence has been juiced out in the reductions. If you're ambitious, it's already difficult to maintain presence because you are restless by nature. We often plan the next thing we want to accomplish before the first thing is actually done.

But the reality is, you will have to eliminate items from your to-do list and trim things that aren't as critical to take up less of your time and mental energy. I know, no one wants to do this, but as we covered in Section One, your brain will thank you. Too much to do contributes not only to the rabbit hole of scarcity thinking or other scarcity-related influences, it also adds to your mental load and decision fatigue from the deluge of micro trade-offs. Now, you know that I am here with you, doing these very same things. I know that just trimming things you don't like, or that don't matter that much, is not going to be enough to ease your strain. So, you can also grow the size of your metaphorical suitcase to pack with more ease and space.

We'll explore a few key fundamentals to reduce your workload and then we'll go into detail about hidden or lesser-known sources of support. Because the reality is, no one does everything well, nor should they try. And we all need and deserve help. This flying solo myth many of us were raised with only undermines us. Again, until the macro systems we live and work in like traditional workplaces truly work for moms, what we can do is adapt our infrastructures to get as much external support as possible while reprioritizing to become a bit ruthless—yep, I said that—about our time and top of the hierarchy needs. As a gentle reminder, this includes things like sleep, stress management, healthy relationships, and learning.

Revisit Your Highest Priorities

Before you can even think about easing your workload, which you absolutely need to do, you need to know what's core for you right now. What on your too-long list of never-done things is mission critical. People tend to freeze when asked this question, because the list of what's important is pretty long. But at any given time, you need to have a clear sense of your very highest personal priorities, outside of your desires for your children. For example, maybe you'd like to start speaking publicly, teach yoga, get promoted, walk for 20 minutes a day, earn your PhD, become a nutritionist, apply for a TEDx Talk, learn to salsa, reduce your anxiety, or commit to a weekly date night with your partner.

To help refine your list, here are two things you need to know:

- Your highest priorities list needs to be two or three things at most.
- The priorities will (and should) change regularly.

By regularly, I mean quarterly, because your environment, responsibilities, and conditions change constantly. What we're being asked to do, directly or indirectly by circumstance, isn't static. If you are blessed with children who follow a typical health and growth trajectory, you're changing what they eat, how you interact with them, what you read to them, how you play with them, where they're educated, and how you explain things all of the time. And it's happening quickly, from liquids to solids, crawling to toddling, from having them following our leads to creating their own unique paths, and then teaching us about everything they see.

Reflect on What You Do Best and Consider Important

I love the book *Drop the Ball* by Tiffany Dufu.[3] One of the many concepts she shared that has stayed with me is her question, "what is my best, highest use?" Another lens on that is what author and clinical psychologist Dr. Gay Hendricks calls your "zone of genius"[4] in your personal life or professional life.

This isn't quite the same as my earlier question about your priorities, which often means goals or aspirations. What you want to accomplish is different from what you are good at and well served doing. A subtle but important distinction as you trim, trim, trim, and eliminate to streamline your time.

For example, teaching my kids to learn new things, playing with them, getting to know them, and even feeding them nutritious foods feels meaningful to me. It's part of my best highest use. But cleaning up after them does not feel that way. So, start to carve out what time with your family or at home fuels you. Now that does not mean that we can eliminate every single undesirable task from the never-done list. But thinking in this way helps you decide where your time priorities really are.

For example, you might really want to throw a birthday party that your children remember. But party planning is not your strength, and all the steps required in the way that you were thinking of it aren't going to fit with your schedule. It might be that you decide to order a cake from a local store or bakery instead of making one. Or you go to a kids' party venue instead of hosting it at your home. Or you order pizzas, instead of making ham and cheese sandwiches that look like windmills. There are lots of ways to create a meaningful celebration and reduce work in the places that don't feel like the "best, highest use" of your time.

During the first year of the pandemic, my husband and I started doing a weekly date night–movie night in the living room, after the kids were asleep. At that point, I hadn't watched television for over three years. Do I like television? Yes. Did I miss it by giving it up? Well not in the way I expected to. When I decided to reclaim my creative energy, and began to write about these topics of stress and self-care and also food and cooking early on, I had to make trade-offs. I had a full-time job and, at the time, a toddler and a kindergartener. There wasn't extra space, I couldn't pack more in, I had to remove things.

And I removed a lot of things, trimming time in places that I could live with. I stopped getting my nails done, and only did them myself, for special occasions. And there was no more doing elaborate things with my hair (hello hair bun or braids), and I streamlined everything about how I was dealing with dinners and cooking, as my favorite hobby had to be restructured and simplified. Think batch-making chocolate banana bread for the kids versus delicate, time-consuming desserts like gateau opera.[5] I was a little sad about that but I was happy to save hours of time that I could repurpose for something more important to me.

There are likely places where you're spending time now that don't feel very healing or fueling to you. Maybe it's television, like it was for me most nights before I returned to creative writing. Or it could be social media. After all, does your friend from middle school need you to "like" every picture of her last vacation? For context, when I feel myself engaging in a doom scroll instead of productive use of social media, which tends to happen when I'm very tired, it's a call to action for me to stop and go to sleep. You may be engaging in commitments you really don't want to engage in. Like driving back and forth to those hours of sports practices for your kid when your partner could have (and would have) done it, driving back and forth to run errands that could have been batched all together so you could take care of them once every six weeks instead of weekly. Or perhaps outsourced to a helper or paid service. Hello TaskRabbit, or local delivery service to return all of those packages with the shoes that don't fit.

Again, think of activities that either drain you or you feel neutral about them. Start there but let your why drive you. If you have those two or three things you *really* want to accomplish this quarter (and remember, you get to change your mind at any point and revisit at least every few months) then it's easier to let other things go that matter less. Because it's not forever. And being more intentional about your highest uses just gives you more energy and tends to be finished more quickly than doing a lot of things you dislike or suck at. Knowing what matters to you most right now also makes it easier to say no to anything that isn't on that priority list.

Notes

1. https://www.ncbi.nlm.nih.gov/pmc/articles/PMC5748336/#R45
2. https://www.amazon.com/Sendhil-Mullainathan-Scarcity-2014-09-19-Paperback/dp/B00PW0UU2Q
3. https://us.macmillan.com/books/9781250071767/droptheball
4. https://hendricks.com/gay-talks-about-taking-the-big-leap-into-the-genius-zone-on-the-inspired-money-podcast-with-andy-wang/
5. https://en.wikipedia.org/wiki/Opera_cake

Chapter 5

Overcome Common Boundary Traps

After circling three times I quickly pulled my car into the only parking space left in the garage. Too quickly because I felt the faintest thump as I opened my door, wedged tight against the much-nicer car parked next to mine. I whispered to myself, "How ridiculous, why, why, why now?" I put the key back into the ignition and pulled backward. I tried to incrementally adjust the car so that it was further over to the right. After investing an extra five minutes that felt like 15, I deemed my parking effort good enough. I inspected the car next to me with my eyes and even my hands. No damage, thank God! After breathing out a small sigh of relief, I pulled the bags hastily out of the back seat and started running to the front door of the building.

I glanced briefly at the stairwell but opted for the elevator. I had just enough time before my first meeting to stop in the mother's room and pump milk. By the time I arrived on the ninth floor, I was panting and started pulling everything out of the bags before realizing, I had left the breast pump at home. Although I'm not someone who typically cries or screams in frustration, if I were someplace really private instead of at my office building, I probably would have. I sent a quick email to my boss, "I'm here in the office but unfortunately, I have to run back home, I forgot something pretty important. I should be back within a couple of hours but will have to dial into our next meeting from the car. Talk soon."

The rest of that day was a blur after stopping at home in excruciating pain to pump milk, I returned to the office for what felt like only a few hours of meetings, before having to leave again. I had a big strategy presentation that I needed to work on, but every day was full of meetings and every night was full of childcare and housework, so I found myself trying to pull it together in the last stretch of the deadline, which had only been issued a couple of days before. In that particular job, unless it was my own strategy for my team, the deadlines were always short.

Later that night, after my daughter went down for the first stretch of her sleep, I frantically opened my laptop while sitting on the floor to prevent the glow of the computer from disturbing the baby. "Candidly, this is subpar." I blinked and my stomach tightened. I reread the email from my boss and bit my lip trying to fight the queasiness fueled by shame and exhaustion. I knew he was right. Between pumping and endless meetings, my strategic work and writing was pushed to nights or weekends. I had started this practice years before but what seemed to work then failed me post-kids. I poured any found time into the email abyss wanting to feel "on top" of something again, even if it was my inbox. I managed a team, so I needed to be available and responsive to them too. Have you ever read Cal Newport's book, *Deep Work*?[1] He coined the phrase to describe focused work that requires our presence, like writing a proposal. Well, my deep work just wasn't coming together at that point.

My thoughts came in distracted threads. Did I return the permission slip to preschool? Do I hear a baby crying . . . is *my* baby crying? Shit . . . forgot to book the mother's room for the morning to pump. Move the meeting, join it late, or pump in the car? Decisions and demands nibbled my time and energy. When I wasn't tired, I was angry with myself and everyone around me for not (seeming) to work as hard as I was. I felt sick about turning in sloppy work and disappointing my boss, who had been an advocate.

I returned from maternity leave three months before that email. You may have heard of the "second shift" for moms, popularized in the book[2] by sociologist Dr. Arlie Hochschild and Anne Machung. Well at that point, my work for an important presentation was pushed to my third or fourth shift because my then infant daughter was sleeping in 90-minute blocks between feedings, in a co-sleeper next to my side of the bed.

My nanny, at the time, had taken a one-month leave of absence to care for her mother who was having major surgery, so I also didn't have childcare. I didn't know at the time; she'd give her notice a couple of months later to move back to Colombia and care for her parents for an extended period. My work troubles only deepened, and although my own mother came to stay and help with the kids as much as possible every time I lost childcare, I failed to keep my fragile postpartum work–life together.

After years of pushing past every barrier to earn a strong professional reputation, somehow, I managed to back myself into a corner and quickly lost my mooring. Despite the importance to my career and team, I wrote a strategy draft that was mediocre at best. The sharp (honest) criticism from my boss, catalyzed a stronger response and I spent many hours that weekend rewriting and ultimately producing an acceptable 25 pages. It was still far from my best and worse, the postpartum mask that was firmly in place at work finally slipped. I exposed a vexing weakness to a critical professional ally.

I was in an all-time energy drought. The welcome, hard-fought addition of my daughter left me emotionally and physically exhausted. The too-swift return into the job I once loved, compounded by the everything-needs-my-attention list lengthening, left me creatively depleted. You may be thinking, "Wait, Leslie, why didn't you ask for more help or explain to your boss what was going on? What about your boundaries?"

"Healthy" work–life boundaries weren't on my radar then. I built my professional reputation and career success, to some extent, from being ultra-responsive. It took a long time before I was motivated enough to create or protect my boundaries. My boss at the time was a lovely man and a dad, but as comfortable as I was with him, I didn't feel like I could share my breastfeeding or exhaustion struggles with enough detail for him to understand how chopped up my work days were.

Now I can look back and reflect on each time I could have, should have, and didn't set a boundary. Or misfired with the wrong type of boundary. Although at the time, of course, none of that was nice and I'm happy I can at least share these lessons with you. I strongly encourage boundary setting and they're important, but the truth is they often fail. Why? Two reasons: (1) in many cases, we are unaware of our boundary triggers and (2) we try to set and keep boundaries in situations where we lack psychological safety or social power.

That particular job held both types of boundary traps for me, especially in the months after my return from leave. Let's unpack this a bit. Because boundaries, one of the most powerful tools in your tool kit to care for yourself, can be used very strategically and successfully. But even if you're a Jedi-level boundary-setting genius, often they don't work in the way we expect, and certainly not for every situation.

We're told, and even taught, to exercise personal power to solve problems. And if you've read any of the most popular self-help books or research, like I have, they give lots of advice about boundaries, often by people who are not moms or don't have your life experience. Despite the well-intentioned and thoughtful information, it's just not the same when you try to implement it. One of my earlier research studies for Mom's Hierarchy of Needs was all about boundary setting and since I've written a lot about this topic, I won't go into every detail here. The important part for you to know is that yes, establishing and keeping personal boundaries, is part of "the answer" to the "never-done" list where we get stuck in cycles of tasks that can't be finished. But the reality is, without an understanding of when and why boundaries fail, it's difficult to make them work for you consistently.

Know Your Personal Boundary Triggers

The biggest barrier to boundary setting or keeping in our boundaries study for moms was how personal and subjective the right conditions are. For example, some people felt like it was easy to set boundaries with people that they knew really well such as close friends because they felt psychologically safe enough to speak the truth. But with others, it was the exact opposite. They were most comfortable setting boundaries when there was no personal relationship; basically, if it's a stranger they thought, "Who cares what they think so, I will assert my preferences." Other people have difficulty setting boundaries when it's related to career growth or a professional opportunity (like me). For example, if you work a sales role or own a business, and you've decided to be home for dinner at least four nights of the week but going to that extra networking event, or client dinner, can advance your financial well-being, it's a tough call.

Another insight from the study was that if you are not in a good place mentally or emotionally, for example, if you're anxious, depressed, or feeling particularly triggered, holding on to your personal boundaries is more challenging when you are rattled. It makes sense but sometimes we forget that feeling bad is another vulnerability, one that's likely to stand between you and self-protection. If someone asks you in that moment whether you can watch their kids, volunteer for that committee, or attend that parent–teacher organization meeting—none of those things that you really want to make the time for—you might be more inclined to say yes. We find ourselves in really dynamic conditions internally and externally, which is why all that traditional advice about holding your boundaries or setting boundaries can fail. But if you start with your triggers and really internalize what is hardest for you—such as the people or contexts where it feels the most difficult, versus when it feels really easy to say no, you suddenly can preempt the challenge.

When Is It Hardest for You to Set or Keep Boundaries?

There is an incredible mom who inspired the Mom's Hierarchy of Needs boundaries research study. I used to see her all of the time at the gym because, back then, I still ran indoors. One day on the treadmill next to me she described how during a business trip when she stayed with her mother-in-law she ended up missing her workouts that she planned to have, eating food that she did not want to eat, and generally not using the time away on the trip to engage in restorative self-care outside of the busy work schedule. Now you could reframe this one, on reflection, to decide that pleasing your mother-in-law is an investment in having the next holiday or family gathering go smoothly or that spending time bonding under her conditions enables you to deepen the relationship, especially if that relationship needs strengthening. There are many good reasons to break your own rules from time to time! But in this case, with this particular friend, she did not feel good about it. She came back from that trip feeling regret, like she had let herself down, and too many of us experience this.

I redistributed our daughter's sports practices and games to my husband, because I'm already overloaded with the school and sports requirements for our son. But every time they have to leave for a soccer game or karate, I find myself filling water bottles, putting equipment into bags, or otherwise micromanaging the entire thing from a mental load standpoint. Why? Well, I've had to think a lot about that. It's mostly because if there's no water or the shin guards aren't on (both of which have happened by the way), my daughter suffers and she's only nine. It feels like an unreasonable consequence to pass along to her, for something that isn't quite age-appropriate for her to be consistently in charge of. By contrast, I'm willing to release mental load fully to my husband, if the consequences of him not remembering to do the prep work hit him directly.

Remember, in our society we are rewarded for being pleasing, but it's bigger than that: women are expected to be self-sacrificing and pleasing. I'm very grateful to my own mother who raised us kids without the expectation that she would be pleasing us. She was then and still is feisty and direct with her point of view. In our home, she was the boss and made it clear while parenting my sister and me that she'd be telling us to do things that we would not want to do, and she didn't expect us to be happy about that. Although my mom paused her career for many years to focus on the home, she was quite vocal and specific with my dad about anything she was disappointed about. Now, a little caveat, as I shared: my parents are from Barbados and there are some cultural expectations that come with Caribbean parenting that don't always map to the US culture. So, depending on where your family is from, how you were raised, what you were taught, and how it was modeled to you, your circumstances might have led you to an entirely different set of expectations about how assertive you can or want to be. This includes how many consequences, if any, you comfortably lay down when people do not respect your boundaries. The beauty of being the mom now is that you get to rewrite rules that work for your life.

If boundaries haven't worked for you traditionally, they still can work for you. You have the opportunity to reflect and adjust as you go.

Let's Review: Boundary Setting and Keeping

> "I often minimize my personal needs boundaries over the needs of my kid or family (e.g., stay up late to finish work, don't take nights off from family, seldom workout because it would mean being away from night routine, etc.)."
>
> "I don't [set boundaries]. I will forever be a people pleaser."
>
> "I realized I was a puppet. I try to not hurt feelings, but often mine were hurt. I have started speaking out more."

These are a few anonymous quotes from mothers who participated in our boundary setting study. Whether it's sometimes or all the time, when we struggle to set boundaries, we often suffer the downstream consequences. Extra helping of emotional labor anyone? Interested in adding more work on top of your existing work?

Right, I'm sure you're thinking "why, no thank you" so I'm going to give you a very brief refresher on boundary setting. When you decide that you are setting a boundary and communicate that you will no longer feed your kids a second dinner if they don't like the one that you made, that your partner cannot ask you non-time-sensitive questions while you are both working from home during your workday, or that you will no longer stay in the office past 5 p.m. when it's completely unnecessary anyway and you are tired of paying those daycare late fines, or whatever "it" is, there has to be a consequence and response if people in your life do not honor the boundary you set.

It might be the consequence is that the thing doesn't get done that you are not willing to do anymore. In the previous examples, the kids must eat the dinner you made; otherwise, they sit for as long as it takes until it's in their bellies; you don't answer the texts from your partner or entertain questions until the end of your workday; and your remind everyone at work that you've blocked off pick-up time on your calendar and are unavailable for meetings or questions. For example, I'm not going to refill the sparkling water pitchers anymore if no one else in the family does, because I don't actually use it. Not ever, I prefer the simplicity of still water so the consequence for someone (ahem, my husband) will be the unpleasant discovery that it's empty when he is very thirsty. Or the consequence is that something else you had planned to do for that person does not get done. For example, "since you didn't pick up the groceries as you promised, then I will not make dinner because it would take an extra hour for me to defrost something and shift the plan. So, you will have to come up with a plan B to feed the family in a reasonable time frame; peace out."

Your story is unique and that's the part you need to honor to make the boundary process really work for you. In our research study, setting boundaries with their children was easiest for most of the moms, whether it's communicating a loss of privileges or some other consequence. Okay, it's probably not a surprise to you that setting boundaries with our kids was the most natural because parenting is, largely, boundary setting. Guiding and teaching young people how to become effective as adults in the future requires setting a lot of limits. And often, the kids do not want to do "it" the way we are trying to show them, or they don't want to do "it" at all. But in the same way you probably won't let your kids eat cake or ice cream for every meal, there are times other people in our lives need to be corrected. Yep, I said that.

Here's what we learned in our study*, which was qualitative in nature but very rich and instructive. More detailed summaries from the series, including "How Moms Can Set Boundaries Without Feeling Guilty"[3] and "What Happens In Your Marriage When You Try to Set Boundaries"[4] are available on the Mom's Hierarchy of Needs website. The three hardest boundary setting conditions were as follows:

State of Mind

When feeling tired and/or overwhelmed	22%
When I feel guilty about not meeting expectations or pleasing others	12%
When I feel scared, anxious, or depressed	3%

Relationship

When the choice affects my kids and/or spouse	20%
When dealing with family of origin	4%
When dealing with in-laws or extended family	4%

Context or Environment

Conflicts with work obligations or opportunities	10%
When under time pressure	4%
When there is a values conflict for an issue/opportunity I feel strongly about	3%
Other (sex/intimacy expectations with partner, maintaining a diet, keeping a budget, feeling unfamiliar with an environment or topic)	18%

Now that you have some sense of where your boundary triggers are—the situations, people, environments, or contexts where you are less likely to keep a firm boundary—you can start to come up with a response strategy. Yes, in every one of those situations, you will need to create a canned response you can turn to when flustered and put into that awkward

---

*189 Mom's Hierarchy of Needs, Boundary Study

scenario that's ill-suited to your boundary-keeping success. You will need to come up with a response for every major boundary trigger. It can be an email template that you save or a note that you keep on your phone, but it'll be a tool that you can use when the situation is particularly trying for you. In the Afterword of the book, I will lead you to some systems guides, where you'll see examples of this in the "when to say yes to a volunteer assignment" item.

Use Boundary Setting When It's Psychologically Safe for You

Back to you and your boundary guidelines. Again, don't get into the weeds of the specific situations I've given as examples, because I want you to create your own boundary rules that work for how you are wired and how your life is.

Perhaps one of the biggest pitfalls we face with boundary setting, even if we are quite good at it and committed to it, is trying to do it in environments where we are not psychologically safe. Hopefully that is not the case in your home. For most of you reading this, home is where you will have the most power and control to reset expectations. If you do not feel psychologically safe or physically safe in your home, that is a bigger concern and one that requires your immediate attention and perhaps additional resources or people, like an employee assistance plan if you have access to one, therapist, or another medical professional such as your primary care doctor to help you.

But if you lack psychological safety in another setting, such as in your workplace, which is common for many, many women, you might feel very confident about setting your boundary only to have it come back to bite you. You can decide that you will not go out of town for work anymore "unless they've given at least one month's notice" to protect your life and childcare from disruption. Or you may decide, and communicate, that you "will not take more than two work trips a month" because of the added childcare costs and disruption to your family life, workouts, or your diet. Even if your requests are very reasonable, and of course they are, it can translate into you not being viewed a "team player" or "committed to the organization" or even committed to your career. Countless studies have shown what many of us experience, that "negotiation bias"[5] exists for women, people of color and those from other historically marginalized groups, like those with disabilities, and members of the LGBTQ+ community. Often, it's studied in the context of compensation, promotions, or other financial negotiations. But boundary setting, for what your time is worth, is a lot like asserting what you're worth professionally. Whether it's with your spouse, your parents, your friends, colleagues, or children, if you are setting a boundary, you are drawing a bright line to highlight what you will and will not do, what your time, energy, or peace are worth. Unfortunately, not everyone around you will acknowledge or even accept it.

Please Note, Boundary Rules Differ at Work

I shared the story of my layoff in Chapter 2 as a cautionary tale. There was a lot happening behind the scenes before I was let go. My standing in the organization was changing, and the level of proactive reputation management and internal networking they expected was changing. There were so many boundaries I didn't set to protect my energy, time, or talent with my leadership team, in part because I didn't really feel psychologically safe anymore, even though I once absolutely did and had loved that company. Work is also one of my boundary triggers. I'm more inclined to override my own good judgment if it means getting accolades or securing an opportunity in my career. I grew up financially insecure; I was raised to view work stability as financial stability and financial stability as my number one priority. I also didn't know how well it would go for me if I started to push back. After all, I had a family at this point, new expenses, and I was physically not at my best after either of my kids were born. Elaine Lin Herring, author of *Unlearning Silence*, described this beautifully when I interviewed her for Mom's Hierarchy of Needs. She said, "What makes conflict so hard to stomach or navigate is that the fallout is so unequally born. Because if I have conflict with my boss, we're not on the same playing field. They still have influence over whether I get promoted, and how tough my life is, if I choose to stay there. There's a cost to raise conflict. It's the cost of not knowing how they're going to react or what the repercussions are. And that cost is all on me."

How Much Personal Power Do You Have?

We know the "-isms" like the sexism that undermines how women are heard, the racism that further undermines how Brown, Black, Indigenous, and other women of color are heard, the "ableism" that discounts the voices of those with disabilities, or bias against members of the LGBTQ+ community are in the backdrop. Basically, you can't effectively stand up for yourself or your boundaries without seeing the undercurrents that affect your power in each situation or setting. We fall into a perilous double bind as women that even when we try to negotiate and use our power to assert ourselves, it can hurt us. Especially in work settings but it's much bigger than that. Because after all people don't expect you to use your full power anywhere, and especially not there. And in most organizations, if you are the employee and they are the employer, most of that power lies with them. Unless you are in a unique type of role or position (and that doesn't mean that you have to be the most senior person), you may hold a position of power in an organization because you have a lot of history or tenure doing that particular job that no one else knows how to do. Or you're independently wealthy, and it's well known that you're there by choice and don't need the job. You may have a very strong personal brand or patent that gives you agency and choice within your industry or field, or it may be a family business, and your family started it. And like me, if you were raised in an immigrant family with a powerful matriarch, you might have bypassed some of this confusing conditioning that happens to women in the United States and other parts of the world in early childhood, only to later experience the difficulty of setting boundaries in certain environments, like work environments, as an adult. Some of these are edge cases but it's important to know there are circumstances that disrupt the imbalance in your favor. And you can use this knowledge to be more effective and selective with your strategies.

When Seeking Flexibility, Don't Assume All Female Leaders Are Automatic Allies

Most of my live interactions with moms, dads, and family caregivers are when their employers hire me. Most of my work with organizations is to help change the workplace for parents and caregivers, often by evolving the policies, benefits, or practices to be caregiver friendly. And the reality is, as I'm sure you well know, not every parent is having the same experience at work. Although by age 44, most women (86%) become mothers, whether they are moms or not, we're still woefully underrepresented in leadership roles. We also know the Fortune 500 has hit a record number of female CEOs at only 10.4%[6] and I don't know if they're all moms or not. These are among the most influential organizations in the world. Although I haven't run the numbers, I suspect most of the male Fortune 500 CEOs are dads. Despite the prevalence of co-, sole, or primary breadwinning women, when partnered with men as reported by Pew Research,[7] "in egalitarian marriages, husbands spend more time on paid work and leisure than wives do." And by extension, wives spend more time on housework and caregiving, regardless of whether they earn more money or spend more time on paid work.

The point here is that you have this whole community of amazing male workers and leaders who often are partnered with a talented woman whom they can completely trust to do all the things at home for their children and households. Not only are they free from a lot of the mental load, they have a different relationship to work and time. And because leaders are still mostly male, at the very top in organizations, there's a shorthand and a language that men use with each other that many women continue to feel locked out of.

The dads I work with, however, also approach me with concerns about their ability to be recognized as parents or caregivers and to have the type of flexibility they need and deserve. Many are eager to spend more time with their children, partners, aging parents, and actively engage with their homes and communities. There are also quite a few single dads. Although it's not the focus of this book, one of our early employer research reports is dedicated to "recognizing dads as caregivers in the workplace," because it remains an overlooked, important, and essential part of the solution for mothers, children, and families.

So, you may be thinking, "wait, I work for a women-owned business" or "my boss is a woman"; why isn't this easier? If you do, that is amazing! What many of us experience, however, is that even when you have a leader who is a woman or a mom no less, she may may have had to internalize and adopt traditional "successful" leadership behavior, which is still largely male behavior, circa the 1950s. Which means, she had to make sacrifices to be where she is professionally and may not give you any grace whatsoever when it comes to helping you honor your own boundaries. I've been fortunate to work with incredible women as managers, mentors, clients, and super connectors. However, in my corporate life most of my sponsors—the people who put the full weight of their social capital behind my promotions, advancement, or stretch assignments—were thoughtful, forward-looking men. So, tread carefully and get a sense of what the stated and demonstrated expectations are with your manager, even if you have a "mom boss" as a boss.

Ask for Resources Up Front

I've had several colleagues do this really well over the years, even though I was usually not the person to do this really well. Here's the scenario. If you approached them with a need and described a project where you needed to involve them or their department, they would smile nod their heads enthusiastically and say, "yes, this sounds like a great project and I would love to have my team involved. Based on what you're describing it probably needs a project manager and one or two other people to support it at half of their time. So, what is your budget? How much can you allocate to this effort? Once you have the resources let's set up a planning meeting and we can get started right away." Okay, did you catch that? There are so many brilliant things about this approach that I love. First you show up positive and excited to support the work effort, while you also demonstrate responsibility and leadership about resourcing and scheduling the project effectively. I realize this doesn't work for every circumstance. It depends on the nature of your work and the type of role and organization you're in. If this strategy fits your situation, the next time you are asked to do something that will require more resources or time, ask up front or offer (with some lead time) to put an estimate together of what it will take.

If You Have a Cross-Functional or Direct Team, Delegate

Even the most senior leader still has someone in the organization they report to. So, you may be a people manager but ultimately, you still have a group manager, C-suite, or board whom you report to. But you are in charge of something, and women aren't always primed to use their superpowers when they are leading a department, team, workflow, or project. You can, however, ease your workload *and* improve career growth for others in a way that is completely sanctioned. I had the pleasure of interviewing Daisy Auger-Domínguez, seasoned human resource exec and author of *From Burnt Out to Lit Up*, for Mom's Hierarchy of Needs about exactly this topic. She said, "We fool ourselves into believing we have to be on 24/7—and to be fair, the world often hits us 24/7 too, right? When I managed a global team, I could have easily spent my entire day glued to my computer, answering emails from colleagues in Europe, Asia, and the Middle East. I didn't manage that well, and that's what led to my burnout. Looking back, I see now that I could have set firmer boundaries and delegated more intentionally."

Delegation, done well and received well, is a beautiful thing. Daisy explained, "In your thirties, you might not have much room to delegate—you're still building those skills, and everyone around you is at a different stage. But by the time you're in your forties and fifties, especially in more senior roles, developing people becomes essential. And developing people means learning to delegate." As managers of people or projects, we're rarely taught how tricky it can be or how to increase and monitor delegation over time. To really maximize the efforts of your team, it does require some up-front relationship building and discovery work. Although you can observe over time what people are best at, you have to speak with them in a safe space to really understand what they struggle with or where they want to go in their careers. This deeper understanding of your team's motivators and needs as individuals enables you to craft assignments that are effective and instructive over time. I've been fortunate to manage a lot of people, but even when I didn't have direct reports, I was naturally drawn to launching projects so I became responsible for cross-functional product launches, which gave me many leadership opportunities. By the time I did mentor my first direct report, when I was in my late twenties, I made many mistakes, especially managing up and with my peers. Nurturing people and helping them grow professionally, however, is a gift and an honor so be intentional with the opportunity when you have it.

Decide If Managing People Works for You

"Leslie, I keep seeing other people getting promoted into these senior leadership roles or roles where they manage a lot of other people. I'm not sure if I want to do that in the next few years, but it seems like the only way to advance." This was a thoughtful email from a member of the Mom's Hierarchy of Needs community. At the time, she was exploring a job change and I've had this conversation many times with people whom I've managed over the years. First, let me spill the tea: many people who manage other people burn out on it. If you find yourself in this position, feeling trapped as a manager of people, ask yourself the following questions:

- Do I like the people on my team?
- Do I trust the people on my team?
- Have I been able to effectively delegate and reassign work to the people on my team, and if not, why not?
- Have I learned anything about the frequency of checking in with others that would make it easier the next time?

- Are there people on my team who are ready for more responsibility?
- Are there people on my team who have stagnated in their roles?
- Do I have too many people reporting to me?
- Am I giving the care and attention to each person who reports to me that they deserve?
- Have I felt more leveraged and able to get significant work done by managing people versus when I did not manage people? If not, why not?
- Have I sought or received professional development support, formally or informally, to grow my managerial skills?

This little quiz is for you to ask yourself, not something you need to share with others. Nor do you need to feel bad about any of the answers. The answers are what they are. What's most important for you to know is you don't have to manage, or want to manage, people; it's not for everyone. As I have discussed with a lot of moms, the mental and emotional energy required to manage people, especially in this very high burnout climate where most of the workforce are still stunned post-pandemic, is tough. Just like raising kids, though, it's extremely rewarding and often enables you to amplify your professional impact.

Please note you can move in and out of being a people manager. We have a broader range of career options and seasons with the rise of flexible, hybrid, or remote work, and part-time or fractional assignments, even as a senior leader. Less rigid structures to adhere to also means fewer binary choices.

Whatever stage you're at in your professional life, if you're not yet leading people or teams, but you're considering the impact it would have on your work and mental load, ask other people in your network, especially moms or other parents and caregivers, how they're doing it: what's working well for them, where they seek support, and what that looks like. As I've told many people privately who are afraid that people management may not be right for them, there are also many paths to being a skilled and highly compensated individual contributor. There are extraordinary salespeople, software engineers, clinicians, teachers, and researchers who do not manage teams but contribute in ways they are happiest and most fulfilled by.

Leadership Assignments Aren't All the Same

Managing a team of 5 is different than managing a team of 15. And if you have 50 or 150 people to manage, you might have only two of those people report directly to you and find the volume is not daunting because you have access to other competent senior leaders. If other senior people are hands-on with daily operations, you may be freed to focus on the big picture, if that's what's in your zone of genius.

My point here is what feels manageable for your workload, especially if that includes managing others, can be very nuanced. It's not just the nature of your work; it's not just whether you like your [fill in the blank here] company, manager, or your industry. It also comes down to how well supported you are.

Set a Time Limit to Working Scrappy (aka Under-Resourced)

If you start to feel the terrible burnout-y feeling, it's tough to recover from quickly. I remember the physical feeling of just being so overloaded because I took on more and more without asking for additional resources in the form of budget or new hires. Remember the China project I shared in Chapter 2? That was one of many in my career because I love being the person who does "the thing" that hasn't happened before. Each time (and, yes, I'll admit it it's happened more than once) when I proved the potential of whatever "it" was that I was working on, I generally received more people or resources. But in hindsight if I had become more attuned to when the workload really required more people to do it well or set up checkpoints along the way to preempt growing needs, I could have asked the organization to invest in that growth. I'm sure I could have avoided a lot of missed sleep and frustration. For example, if you're assigned to project X, and you know it could blossom into something big and beautiful workwise, but you're starting without any resources, speak up! "I'm so excited to start this new project! Let's align on how its success will be measured and when there are early signs of progress, how quickly additional resources can be hired or brought in. If we are gaining momentum but the resources aren't available, we can agree how to pause or shift the schedule until it can be staffed appropriately."

How to Identify What Needs Delegation or Reassignment

If you manage people or have influence over other people's work as a project or process manager, let's start trimming your work right now. Yes, as in today. Please identify that list of things that are prime delegation targets. Then, create three columns at the top of an old-school sheet of paper or on a document and name them.

Name the first one "I don't have time to do this effectively." The second one is "I shouldn't be doing this at all" and you know what I'm talking about: that odd task that ended up in your team because a former employee used to do it and then it was rolled over the fence to you. Or it's a project that's either way out of scope for your role or way outside of your personal zone of genius. And the third one is "things that maybe no one at all should do." Like that report that takes hours that no one ever looks at, scheduling that meeting that barely anyone attends, providing status updates every month on that thing that no one cares about this year. The larger your organization and longer your tenure, the bigger these lists will be.

On another virtual or physical sheet, create a fourth list of things that you can do in your sleep you're so seasoned at but realize those tasks or projects are not in your best interest to hold onto. They don't belong with you, should move into another group, or you can teach and reassign them to another person on the team. Think about those first two lists—do you need "approval" to get rid of these projects or reassign them? Can you just announce that it has happened or silently sunset something that no one outside of the team needs information about?

As the very wise Daisy shared, management = delegation, my friend! Growth for others comes from learning new things and taking on more (or different) responsibilities. And that's growth and freedom for you to take on more if you're in a season where you want that. You might want to rest more and breathe more; you get to choose what to do with the extra time, but look for that space and don't just fill it up right away. Savor it and choose strategically how to use it.

Use Group Power Instead of Personal Power When It's Not Psychologically Safe

When it's not your call or it may be but you're dealing with office politics (aka microaggressions), sometimes the best strategy to overcome a lack of psychological safety in the workplace or any other system is to use the collective power of a group. This works in other settings as well where you may be trying to make a change, such as in your co-op or condo building, school system, neighborhood, or faith-based community. Basically, wherever you are part of a larger, entrenched system, you are more likely to succeed with the support, wisdom, and activation of others.

This works really well with employee resource groups (ERGs) if you need to set or keep boundaries in the workplace. Not every organization has such as group, but if you can't leverage a formal ERG for parents or caregivers, an informal group of other parents and caregivers can be as effective. And it doesn't only have to be women, if we're talking about caregiving or parenting, ideally involve men, too. The emotional, physical, and societal cost of care is disproportionately owned by women today, but hopefully it will not be this way in the future. I once described "feminism 2.0" as a bit like becoming a soldier in a war you never signed up for and didn't know existed. Until I had children, the deep inequities we face as mothers were invisible to me. Sometimes we have to straddle improving our lives right now, with the reality of evolving the systems and culture for the long term in ways that our children and grandchildren will benefit from. This book, as I promised you, is not about the systems side of my work but we will go there sometimes to help you navigate and use the strategies for your life right now. Because you deserve and need support in the present moment.

The power of a group can help you do the following:

- Understand what the culture has delivered to date to other people with similar needs, so you can problem-solve with more data and stories within your organization or community. For example, in the next caregivers group meeting for your employer, you can ask, "I've had a hard time protecting space in the calendar to leave work and pick up my kids on time. Have any of you had similar struggles and talked with your manager about it? If so, how have you done it?" Or you could say to a group of trusted colleagues, "I'm about to go out on maternity leave and more than half of my compensation is in sales commissions. I'm a bit worried about how going on leave will affect my income. Do you know any other parents who've taken leave from the sales team whom I could speak with?"

- It helps when you can make an ask, as a group, for the conditions you really need, especially when it has to do with work–life integration and equity. For example, "on behalf of the parenting ERG we wanted to share that right now there are only two rooms allocated for breastfeeding but in light of the size of our growing organization we have had to wait to get into the breastfeeding room or go pump milk in our cars. We'd like to suggest adding two more rooms and coming up with a ratio of the number of employees to the number of rooms so that in the future other moms or birthing parents will not run into the challenges that we did." Within the safety of a supportive group, it is no longer you as an individual who needs a specific accommodation or benefit, it is a group of constituents who are part of the same community, asking for a systemic change. And that is powerful stuff.

Have a Canned Response for Your Common Boundary Triggers

When you say yes but really want to say no, what does that look like? I know if my family of origin ask me to do something, even when I don't want to, I'm more likely to say yes. As I shared previously, I'm prone to overcommitting myself on professional opportunities because of the post-traumatic stress disorder from financial instability and wanting to secure my career life and income. I have a link to a systems guide for you in the Afterword that's specifically about volunteering your time. It's so good! There are lots of great examples for that scenario that we so often tend to get stuck in. But for other types of more personal examples you will need to create your own script you can use and reuse.

An example is when you see someone you really like to talk with but you don't have time for it. "It's really great to see you and I know we need to catch up properly but right now I'm on my way into work and I'm trying to get some extra time before my first meetings. Can we set up some time to catch up on one of these weekends instead?" Or perhaps it's health related, "You know I'm a complete chocoholic and that type of cake is my favorite, but I made the commitment this year to eat healthier and really focus on reducing sugar and eating foods that fuel my energy over the long term. So, as much as I love your desserts I have to pass."

Of course, boundary setting and managing the scope of projects at work is a common challenge, and there's a linked systems guide for that in the Afterword also. Here's a possible reply you can tailor for your own use: "I would absolutely love to work on this project. It's the type assignment of that is right in my zone of excellence; however, I'm about to go on vacation and if I start working on this before I leave I will feel compelled to finish it on vacation. I just don't have enough time. I'm so sorry. Might I recommend you talk with X, Y, or Z person who has the right skill sets and could support you in my absence?"

I'm a big fan of using these little scripts in the notes app on my phone or saving them in a file with a document called *boundary setting*. Then you have them at the ready so that you can pop them up and look at them when you need to or copy and paste into an email or text response when you need that polite and thoughtful way to say no. Like when you (or one of your children) are invited to a party you don't want to go to, are asked to produce completely useless documentation at work, or are given a not-so-subtle request to mail something to a family member. You know those things that you keep getting asked for! Okay, now is the time. Take five minutes to write out your own scripted response. For example, "I really love the idea of sending the clothes my kids have outgrown to other children in the family but the amount of time it takes to find a box and stand in line at the post office is too much at this stage of my life. I donate our gently used clothes to local nonprofits and feel great about doing so." See? Super quick because it doesn't have to be fancy. Put this first one into an email (to yourself) save it as an email template or use your notes app then it's ready to save you mental energy the next time that repeated request comes your way.

Notes

1. https://calnewport.com/deep-work-rules-for-focused-success-in-a-distracted-world/
2. https://penguinrandomhousehighereducation.com/book/?isbn=9780143120339
3. https://momshierarchyofneeds.com/how-can-moms-set-boundaries-without-feeling-guilty/
4. https://momshierarchyofneeds.com/what-happens-in-your-marriage-when-you-try-to-set-personal-boundaries/
5. https://www.pon.harvard.edu/daily/leadership-skills-daily/counteracting-racial-and-gender-bias-in-job-negotiations-nb/
6. https://fortune.com/2024/06/04/fortune-500-companies-women-ceos-2024/
7. https://www.pewresearch.org/social-trends/2023/04/13/in-a-growing-share-of-u-s-marriages-husbands-and-wives-earn-about-the-same/

Chapter 6

Get Strategic with Your Childcare Support

"Hi, Robert!" my son said, smiling and waving at the camera as he popped his head over my shoulder. "Hi!" Robert waved back enthusiastically, causing my son to giggle before running back over to my mother, who was trying to gently detangle wet knots from my daughter's very full and very curly head of hair.

I muted myself and stood up from the small, tiki-themed table. "Mum, can you try to keep him over there?" She was intensely focused on my daughter's hair but nodded vaguely at my request. At this point, my beloved nanny whom I mentioned previously, had left. She returned to her home country for several months of fully insured medical treatments that cost a fraction of what they would here in the United States. So, once again, I was searching desperately for someone new, in the midst of an intense season at work.

Robert, my primary point of contact at our strategic partner's company, was getting pretty used to seeing me on video calls from swim school, with the chaos of running children, faux palm trees, and my mother in the background.

Although mum flew in to save the day as usual with her one-way ticket and promise of grandmother care, I was still feeling squeezed. She was in her late seventies at this point, and my children at four and eight were super active. A little too active for her to fully keep up with, so I went with her to swim lessons, dance classes, and any place where keeping eyes on both kids would be more challenging. Ultimately, we hired a wonderful nanny but there was about a two-plus-month gap in coverage this time that my mother graciously covered as she had so many times before. Now, I know how very lucky I am to have a mother who was willing, able, and healthy enough to be our back-up nanny with practically no notice. But childcare, no matter how expensive it is or isn't, and how well organized you are about obtaining it, will fail. And you need support for all the things. In this section of the book, I'll focus on the responsibilities that take up a lot of emotional and calendar space, like childcare. And these responsibilities are more difficult to renegotiate, because they live in environments where our boundaries aren't always honored. In most families moms are still on point for the overwhelming majority of the childcare and household responsibilities, that never-done list of our very highest priorities in the bottom two-thirds of the Mom's Hierarchy of Needs framework. They're the responsibilities we prioritize and value the most, for good reasons. After all, ensuring that the next generation is healthy, happy, and whole is sacred work and it's what we're all here for.

What I am going to do is try to convince you that you don't have to be the sole curator and owner of every single thing related to your children's well-being and care for your home. And that, ideally, it's shared. If you are partnered, please share this responsibility with your partner and if your partner is a man, do so as equitably as possible. But the gendered divide runs deep. Statically speaking, not just in my research studies but in all studies, women do at least twice as much childcare or household work as their male partners, again if partnered and when their partners are male. The *New York Times* reports, in "How Same-Sex Couples Divide Chores and What It Reveals About Modern Parenting,"[1] that "dozens of studies of gay[2] and lesbian couples[3] have found that they divide unpaid[4] labor in a more egalitarian way.[5] They don't have traditional gender roles to fall back on, and they tend to be more committed to equality." However, the article goes on to share in more recent studies that the equitable split in responsibilities at home can shift for same-sex couple's post-kids to create more career space for the higher wage earner. Again, for moms married to dads, studies have shown that the division in household labor is gendered. Regardless of how much money moms make (or don't make) she will still do more household and childcare. I'm operating from what is statistically true for most moms but realize that your life might be completely different. Maybe you are single and have an entirely different set of rules that have been pre-negotiated with a co-parent, or you are not the primary child caregiver. For example, I have met and interviewed incredible women with partners who paused their careers to become the primary caregivers to their children. I also have interviewed incredible women who moved close to their families of origin, or stayed in their hometowns and have abundant access to grandparent care, sometimes from two sets of grandparents! If that is your situation, choose your own adventure and skip the section on childcare and/or the following section about other sources of support.

Childcare Is More Than Baby and Toddler Care

The type of childcare you and your children need depends a lot on their ages, independence, and health. Not every family is blessed with children who become more independent;

millions are caring for children with complex medical needs, chronic illnesses, or disabilities. I won't delve into the detailed difference in special needs care in this book, because having spent some of my time working in the childcare and eldercare industries, to do the topic justice would require its own book. If you are fortunate to have children who follow many of the expected behavioral and growth milestones, then your childcare options will shift from the infant and toddler stages, to what happens in the elementary, middle, and even high school years. And the term *childcare* is being used broadly in this section to mean supporting what your kids need, even if these kids can go into the fridge and find their own snacks. Because childcare, as you well know, isn't only about bathing, feeding, and toileting; it's emotional, logistical, academic, and transportation support because children are not fully independent for a very long time. And many of you with older children are carving out significant emotional space to support their journeys in adolescence and young adulthood. So in this section, I'll focus on your options for nontraditional support that aren't always known or obvious. Because I've written so much about traditional and primary childcare over the years on Mom's Hierarchy of Needs and its information you likely already know, even if you're just getting started with your journey as a mother.

Be Strategic About Your Primary Childcare Coverage

If you live in the United States, you already know that childcare is a mess here. It's expensive, and it's often inaccessible even when people can afford it. There was never enough money in the system of childcare in the United States because it's largely a private, disorganized ecosystem that lacks public funding, with some exceptions at the state level or through schools in underserved communities for early childhood education and Pre-Kindergarten. So, to spare you a long diatribe about childcare when you probably just want to understand how to make it work for you, we'll return to what it is you need.

If you're in the paid workforce, you need childcare. Even if you're not in the paid workforce, you will still need it occasionally. You need the very best childcare that works for you, your family, and your life circumstances. Please note that may differ from what works best for someone else. Hey, can you tell I'm super opinionated about childcare? Here's why: I used to work in the industry, had visibility to how it's set up behind the scenes and a front row seat to how it tends to fail both families and paid caregivers here in the United States. And my mother, for a time in our childhood, worked as a nanny and house cleaner. About three years ago, my sister received a message on LinkedIn and it turned out to be the "baby" mum took care of when my sister and I were kids. He's of course a grown man now with his own kids. Mum happened to be with me when he tracked my sister down and he called my mother to thank her for being such a positive influence and caregiver in his life. So, caregivers are important and even when it's not you, the type of care you select matters.

Most of the time, when the topic or questions about childcare come up, women will err on the side of needing less than what they really need. And just about everyone around them, will try to convince them that they should have as little childcare as possible for the shortest duration possible. This is not suggested out of any malice. This is about the ingrained, often unconscious belief that moms should do everything because we live in a culture that penalizes dependence. So, well-intentioned people who love you will see that you are run into raggedy-land, yet they will still insist that you keep everything on your to-do list. It cannot be both ways.

Factor in Mental Complexity as Another Childcare Cost

At a very high level Table 6.1 gives you a sense of the relative mental load trade-offs in different childcare options. Not every mom wants to use outside childcare, nor can every mom receive it or afford the paid options. It's probably not at all surprising that the options that appear more cost-effective are higher in mental load. But, please note, there are *big* caveats, including the reality there is no 100% perfect, fail-proof childcare.

Table 6.1 Comparison of Childcare Options

Primary Childcare Options	Low Mental Load	Medium Mental Load	High Mental Load
Partner	X		
Your parents/family	X		
Nanny/au pair (live in)	X		
Nanny/sitter (live out)		X	
Full time center-based (daycare/Pre-K)		X	
Part-time center-based (i.e., daycare/Pre-K)			X
Full-time school + afterschool program(s)			X
Full-time school + babysitter/part-time nanny		X	
Full-time school + your partner	X		
Full-time school + family member (your parents/family)	X		
Full-time school + full-time paid caregiver (nanny/sitter)		X	

Understand That All Childcare Fails

If you've had kids for more than a minute, you know none of these options will be available to you 100% of the time, and I'll repeat this because we all are raised to think that careful planning prevents disaster. And, by extension, that when we face problems of any kind, we probably just didn't plan carefully enough. It's just not true.

But some of you reading this are pregnant and planning ahead, or you've paused your career and are ready to resume, or you're dissatisfied with your current childcare setup and plan to upgrade.

So, although it's obvious, let's start with the following truths:

- Nannies, grandparents, and partners will get sick sometimes or need extended time off for other reasons.
- Young people without children can at any time be called into caregiving service for their own parents or grandparents in need.
- Daycares will not care for children who are sick, and you still have to pay for them.
- Au pairs also get sick or homesick sometimes and need to return to their home countries.

School is educational but school is not childcare. Schools are in session on average, for 180 days per year. Yes, you read that correctly. If you've been patiently waiting until your little cutie pie is ready for kindergarten, anticipating huge relief and cost savings, it just isn't so, unless you are also a schoolteacher, which of course, would make school great childcare for you, provided it's on the same schedule as the school or district you work for. If you're not a teacher in the K–12 school system, then your child's school will be closed or unavailable more often than your career will allow, including over the very long stretch of summer when most American parents are playing camp-a-palooza plus using their vacation time to make it work. And afterschool programs often follow school schedules.

I've characterized partner sourcing or family (aka grandparent care) as low mental load because even if there is some friction between you and the family members who care for your child(ren), family members are typically less expensive. Notice I don't say free because you and I know that there is no "free" when someone is doing something for you, whether they are paid directly or not. But family have the agency and authority to fully act in your child's best interest and would throw themselves in front of a speeding train on behalf of your children. There's really no amount of money that can buy that. So, with that said, I realize that grandma may give the kids too much sugar, or your partner (if you are partnered and fortunate to have one who wants to provide the childcare) may allow the kids to have more screen time than they are typically allowed to. Or that your children's clothing may not match in the way you would match them, or as my mother used to say, my sister and I looked like Barabbas[6] whenever my father did our hair. Whatever your concerns are, it's okay. But keep your eyes on the prize! Unless you worry that a family member is not a suitable, values-aligned, or safe option, a less stressed parent means less stressed kids, and that has been validated by many studies.

And if you're feeling guilty about not spending every moment with your child, please read my articles about mom guilt on MomsHierarchyofNeeds.com or the article "Is Good Childcare the Answer to Better Mental Health?"[7] That topic is too big for me to address fully in this book. But the net is, if you are choosing to grow in your career, care for your health, and give your children the advantages that come from financial stability or a fulfilled mom who is choosing to be part of the paid workforce, you are likely trading off something that makes you uncomfortable. Not being around our kids 24/7, although generally speaking is healthy for everyone involved with the right childcare, doesn't always feel good. After the pandemic lockdown, where my kids were home doing Zoom school for 18 months, I felt stressed about them being back in the physical school building, which by the way, was practically across the street from where we live. Why? Well, even though I knew it was in their best interest and that schooling from home did not work well for either of my children, I just feel a greater sense of ease when they are within my arms' reach. It was emotional, not logical. My sister will soon be an empty-nester as her youngest applies to colleges, and this completely terrifies her! There are some scientific reasons for this, too. However, just know the fact that you feel this pull toward having them with you is absolutely okay. But please don't let that natural mama pull prevent you from having reliable, adequate childcare that is within the realm of what you can afford and arrange. Note, childcare costs more than mortgages in most US cities, including mine. So, grandparent care or spouse care might be what is available to you, even if it's not what you would necessarily choose.

My main point here is that there are no wrong answers about what works in your life. But I have had brilliant moms navigating community involvement, going for tenure, deciding to take a C-suite-level position, or choosing to go back to school all feel guilt when asking me about upgrading or establishing their childcare arrangements. Other people (including in some cases their own spouses, who happened to be male spouses in these examples) thought it was "too expensive." So until we spoke about a strategy that made sense for their goals, they paid for the lack of childcare they really needed in the form of the mental energy to stitch together a series of after-school classes, summer camps, negotiate playdates and favors, have their work meetings interrupted, or declining travel and promotions. Don't let this be you. Let the reason that you have the childcare arrangement you have be because (1) you and your partner (if partnered) feel aligned and clear on the cost and benefits and (2) you're choosing the lowest complexity and mental load option you can afford that suits your children. Okay? So, off my soapbox and back to you.

Secret (Underused and Lesser Known) Childcare Options

Whether it's because your mother-in-law is sick, school has closed again, you need to finish your dissertation, train for the marathon, or want a weekly date night, there are many occasions when you will need additional childcare. And it's not always obvious what your options are. Most of us just say no to that thing we had planned when our childcare fails at the last minute. Or when we're considering a stretch opportunity that requires focused time outside of our typical work or coverage hours we often remove ourselves from consideration. The good news? It doesn't have to go down like that, not necessarily. You may have additional options for short-term and occasional coverage.

Country Clubs, Large Hotels, Resorts, and Athletics Facilities

A member of my fabulous team shared that she and her family visit the same resort in Aruba most years for two reasons. One, they plan the trip when another family they are very close with whose kids are the same ages can go so their children have built-in vacation playmates during the visit. And two, it has a really good kids club. So, she and her hubby can use time on their vacation to recharge and rest while the kids play and enjoy a wide range of children's programming. So, of course, most of us don't live in spots like Aruba. But, this concept can work for you in other places, especially if you happen to live in a major metro area or popular destination.

I had a wonderful interview with my former executive coach, Tara Nicholle-Kirke, who also happens to be a single mom, about navigating the dreaded yet familiar mom guilt, while growing professionally. During our video calls I noticed she was always in the same fabulous setting. She explained it was a local country club where she became a member, primarily for its childcare and extensive children's programming. So she was able to go there, work out, and carve additional time to get her work done while her daughter, a preschooler at the time, played in the kids' club. Even if a country club is not within your financial or physical reach, many larger fitness centers and gyms, especially if they cater to women, have childcare available on request, usually for a reasonable fee. If your local community has a YWCA or YMCA, many of these have extensive children's programs, swim lessons, and even after-school and school vacation week programs. YWCAs/YMCAs are not nearly as posh as country clubs but they're well-appointed and much more accessible geographically and financially. So, yes get in that workout but you can also set things up to add a deep work block with the beauty of Wi-Fi everywhere. Imagine a three- or four-hour stretch where your child gets to play, and you can take some time to care for yourself or manage your paid workload.

Faith-Based Programs (Church School, Youth Groups, Synagogues)

Many churches, synagogues, and other faith communities have children's programming. My kids are in Sunday School for an hour before church starts for the adults on Sundays. I typically use that time to go for a later run than I do on Saturday mornings when I'm spinning around with their sports schedules. If you belong to a faith community, you may also have access to programming during school vacation weeks, summers, or at other peak times of the year. Many faith-based facilities also have preschool programs in the same building. Of course, the preschool or daycare facilities will cost money but depending on your community, these programs are often less known, and can have more availability than the larger, daycare programs. You may not even need to be a member of that particular faith community to avail yourself of its paid childcare options, which is true for many faith-based community daycare or after-school programs. Basically, if you're searching for center-based care, leave no stone unturned, and explore the range of possibilities in your local community.

After-School Youth/Apprenticeship Work Programs (for Teens)

If your child(ren) are tweens or teens, you're probably not thinking about "childcare" because they don't need someone to feed them and attend to their every need, but they certainly cannot drive themselves around, nor can they necessarily take care of their meals (proper meals, not snacks), organize their own schedules, answer the school's many emails, find enrichment activities, or navigate complex problems or social dynamics. So, caring for tweens and teens who follow typical health milestones are often forgotten about. We tend to think that once children are out of diapers—okay, maybe I thought this back when my kids were still in diapers—they'd be running their own small empires, but really, it's just not so. There is some exhausted mama ensuring those college applications have been sent in, that after-school job has been applied for, that homework is getting done, those medical appointments have been set, and their mental health and social media use are within an acceptable range. No, I'm not throwing any shade on dads. Of course there are dads who are actively involved in these things, too. And more and more of the dads I meet with, especially on the employer side of my work, are eager and interested in hands-on parenting. But, statistically speaking it's still overwhelmingly moms, as I shared, who are making these types of arrangements, which is why this book is for you. But it doesn't have to be this way, and if your child is older and you are partnered, this is a perfect opportunity to involve your partner. Perhaps your partner was not as involved in your child's baby, toddler, or younger years as you would have liked. But now that the work has shifted to be logistical, strategic, and emotional support, basically training to get your child to a healthy self-sufficient young adulthood, consider sending an SOS to your partner (again, if you are partnered) or to other family members if you are lucky to have a local family. But even distant family can assist with reviewing college essays, as I have been happy to do for my older nieces. Distant family can assist with checking in on your tween or teen, and if they want to be really involved, they might help with paperwork and scheduling madness.

We often set and forget how the roles and responsibilities are arranged in our homes. It doesn't serve us to do so all of the time. Things will continue to evolve and you need more space to yourself, remember? Yes, I won't forget so you won't forget. Don't take any newfound freedom from a task and repurpose it automatically into doing something else in service to everyone else. Ask, remind, and strategically plan for other people to share the joy of raising healthy and happy kids right up until they are earning their full-time salaries and nicely settled into their own homes. I'm not trying to freak you out, but I now see that this parenting thing we do takes a very, very long time and the intensity increases as our children grow and their schedules begin to resemble constellation charts.

Each stage of their lives creates new opportunities for meaningful work experiences, educational opportunities, and other developmental opportunities. So be strategic about lining those up in ways that are appropriate for your child's age, health, and independence. Then your tween, teen, or young adult is getting what they need developmentally, and you have coverage and know that they are being cared for and that their time is being well spent. Although my daughter is nine as I write this, my son started high school this year! Our pediatrician said to me recently, "the key with teens is to keep them busy, and not to allow for too much idle time that can be misspent." This is advice I am taking to heart at this important but fragile stage.

Childcare Collaborations (Pods and Swaps with Neighbors and Close Friends)

Remember when neighborhood pods were all the rage during the height of lockdown? This is still a brilliant option and now doesn't have to be set up to replace the public school system. You and your neighbors can be intentional with an after-school pod, creating structure for transportation, going to or from playgrounds, parks, roller rinks, public pools, or other enjoyable activities. Or choose to kick it old school and be the cool place for the kids to hang out, with some accessible snacks, toys, and games, depending on the ages, stages, and independence of the children involved. You might want to coordinate sharing watching the kids, or perhaps even chipping in the shared cost for an after-school sitter or aspiring teacher to run a group activity. Creating a little bit of structure for a local option reduces the emotional burden for adults and tends to be super fun for kids once your children are later in the elementary school stage, when sports, performance arts, and other programming becomes more frequent and logistically complicated. Finding those other parents whose child(ren) are also part of (insert the blank that fits for you here) soccer/tennis/track/karate/the school play/chorus will help ease the strain because the after-school schedule in itself becomes one of the bears you begin to wrestle on nights and weekends. Of course, these programs are really meaningful for our kids, and we're committed to helping them find their sources of joy and remain physically and intellectually stimulated. But I'm not going to lie to you; it gets really, really hard because these programs are generally uninterested in how easy or difficult it will be for you to make it all happen. Whether you are in the paid workforce, or doing mountains of unpaid work, you will be asked to do random things at random times, often with little notice, that can completely uproot your professional schedule. Which is why, I am also advocating that you consider some form of paid childcare much longer than other people will tell you that you need it. Please study that chart with your options, if you are not yet at the next stage of what you will need. Otherwise, you will be happier creating arrangements with two or three other parents whom you trust, especially if there's driving involved, and when you've had some candid conversations about expectations and safety. And just a little reminder is that when you are happier, your kids are going to be happier, too. When you are unhappy, even if it's not immediately visible, it will make your kids less happy so let's end the culture of self-sacrifice. It's often based on this belief that when we allow ourselves to be miserable doing too many things that at least our kids are getting the best of X, Y, or Z. But the data shows when our cortisol (aka the stress hormone that left unchecked can cause inflammation and all types of other chronic disease) is elevated, then it tends to roll to our children, which nobody wants.

Take Advantage of Lesser Known (or Used) Employee Benefits

Back-Up Caregivers

I worked in the childcare and eldercare industry and learned a lot about back-up care, and to be very candid, even though I had access to it through some of my past employers, it wasn't on my radar until my youngest child was born. This option may not be on yours either. The use rates for this great benefit and most other voluntary employee benefits are shockingly low. If you work for a larger organization, or if you are married and your spouse does, it's very likely that you have what is called *back-up care*, which provides access to childcare (or eldercare) with vetted caregivers you can book on short notice, for a brief period, like a day or even a week. There are many advantages to back-up care; it doesn't just have to be used when your primary childcare fails, although that's its main purpose. For example, I shared the example of using it when our nanny was out for her husband's surgery. Although it can be scheduled the same day, or the day before, it's particularly suitable for those many school closures we know about in advance, such as those teacher professional development days and observance days that most of us still have to work through. So if your children are school-aged, you can take a peek at that school calendar now (yes, put the book down take a peek before any of those odd days come up and surprise you), then go ahead and request your back-up care coverage today. Like all things childcare related, it's imperfect, and although it's intended to be used last minute, it tends to work best when you plan, especially during peak times such as school vacation weeks and summers when it is often much harder to find back-up caregivers. The other problem with childcare and eldercare in the United States is that there are not enough caregivers. It's an under-professionalized industry with many caregivers who work "under the table" so they lack many basic worker protections like workers comp if they have an injury on the job, Social Security to assist with their expenses in their later years, or access to national or state-run health care. If you're working under the table and you are not able to prove that you are paying taxes and have documented wages, you're locked out of a lot of important support. I could write an entire book about this but what is important for you to know is that if back-up caregivers are available to you, planning ahead will serve you. Most of the larger providers, one of which I used to work for, have this available for both childcare and eldercare. However, if you have children with special needs or complex medical needs or adults who require care, it's harder to find paid caregivers in general, and the pool is that much smaller for back-up caregivers with these credentials. But what's beautiful about back-up care is that it's heavily subsidized by most employers; it's typically available for up to 20 days per year, so it will often cost you as little as $8 to $10 per hour in the United States. For those of you who live outside of the United States, you probably have better public policies supporting parents and caregivers. My cousins in Barbados have had entirely different experiences than I have as mothers starting with on average 9- to 12-month maternity leaves versus the piddly 12 weeks that I received. And I realize how lucky I am to have had even that because there are many mothers in this country who go back to work within two weeks of giving birth, often because they lack protected paid leave.

You Can Use Back-Up Care for Self-Care

Mmmmm hmmmm, that's right. You can also use your back-up care benefit for your own self-care. So, if you're single or if your partner isn't available when you're sick, recovering from surgery, or in need of a mental health day, a back-up caregiver could be a great option. If you travel for work with your child, having a caregiver in the city where you're traveling to assist you with coverage would be amazing. I wish I had known about back-up care when I was doing as much travel as I was, especially internationally. I brought my son with me and found local childcare to assist after doing a lot of research and outreach to my Chinese colleagues, but it would have been so much easier to just arrange local back-up care coverage to take care of him while I was in meetings from our hotel. Even though my husband was there, he was also working.

Most of these services provide eldercare as well and I wish I arranged for this after my mom had knee surgery when she was living with my sister and needed a lot of hands on help. It would have been a really cool thing to have a back-up caregiver in addition to the physical therapy and other medical services that she was receiving during that two-month window when her mobility was limited.

Digital Health Platforms with Fertility, Pregnancy, Postpartum, Parenting, and Children's (and/or Adult and Eldercare) Support

Moms are overwhelmingly, the chief medical officers in families. Studies show we're in charge of family health decisions 80% of the time,[8] which I'm sure does not surprise you. We become experts in reading their body language from our child's earliest days. We learn to distinguish the food cry from the diaper change or tired cry and know they're sick long before the thermometer confirms it. Caring for their health is a huge investment we make in our children, and in many cases for our parents and partners as well. A big part of this oversight includes the research to find the right thing, whether it's a diagnosis, treatment, specialist, protocol, clinical trial, or just stylish bandages.

Many of us do or will have kids that need access to specialists and have medical needs that intersect with their mental, physical, and emotional health, including support for neurodivergent children with ADHD, dyslexia, or mental health conditions like anxiety or depression. Basically, all of these conditions are incredibly common and so complex to support, the energy required can completely unravel the most buttoned-up among us. Consider this is a very light dive into this topic because it's not the focus of this book, but I've interviewed great experts over the years who have specialties in this area for Mom's Hierarchy of Needs—like child psychologists, pediatric psychiatrists, and general practitioners and pediatricians. I also did a stint working for a children's mental

Get Strategic with Your Childcare Support

health startup, which gave me access to an incredible group of doctors and experts to learn from. This section is focused on easing the time you spend on health-related navigation. You know, the all-out-love-driven sleuthing you've become so awesome at for everything your children need or will possibly want in the future. It's that research and project management of health care, childcare, and their education that consumes so much of your mental load and emotional labor.

If you are a doctor or health care specialist, then maybe you are the best person to do this work. But if you're not, this is something to consider spouse sourcing if you are partnered. I repeat . . . unless you are a medical professional, consider spouse sourcing if you are partnered! You can turn over setting up and attending doctor's appointments, finding and vetting therapists, reaching out to the school about behavioral health or IEP plans to your partner. And if you are not partnered, or if it's not an option for your partner to become involved, you can consider outsourcing to a specialist or working with one of the great navigation-oriented sites that provides a list of specialists on speed dial for parents to reduce some of the workload. I've included a short list in a few paragraphs with brief summaries as a resource guide to get you started, but it's by no means exhaustive. Many of these services are available through employers so check with your human resources department to first to see if there are parent or caregiver benefits available to you.

Part of the pandemic's great revolution on work–life needs was an increase in companies spending money to support parents, and not just those cool services like breast milk shipping and storage (although those are really great things that I wish I had access to because I traveled a ton postpartum) but spending money on other types of parenting benefits, including telehealth companies with family-focused offerings and services that offer parent coaching, pregnancy, or guidance and sometimes more extended support to find specialists.

When you observe a behavior with your child and you can't get support through your pediatrician or primary care provider, for example, you need to find somebody who knows how to help get your baby to latch just right, your toddler to potty train, or teen to self-manage their homework, or any of those really essential services. Take a close look at the voluntary benefits available to you through your employer. Or again, if you are partnered and have benefits through your partner's employer, look at what they have too because you might be surprised at the services you can access for free or at very low cost. Yes, and you do not have to pay to do some of that navigation if you have access to people on speed dial who know how to find this information and can help you with shortcuts to schedule hard-to-find specialists or surface resources that you would not have been aware of.

Such services fall into a pretty wide yet emerging area, and I've listed a few here to give you a sense of what is possible:

- Massive platforms like Amwell[9] and Teladoc[10] allow you to get quick access to virtual visits and, in some cases, in-person doctors or specialists.
- Specialty platforms focused on parent, children, and family support like Maven Clinic[11] and Carrot Fertility (https://www.get-carrot.com/) and Midi Health provide access to fertility, menopause, postpartum, and other women's health services.

Get Care Navigation Help Courtesy of Your Pediatrician

So, this game-changing tip is from pediatrician, educator, and author of *Parent Like a Pediatrician*, Dr. Rebekah Diamond during an interview for Mom's Hierarchy of Needs.[12] "I know we're very busy and love having single appointments or telehealth visits to discuss one issue. But that issue can also be resources. So, if you're thinking, 'I have to wait until the next well visit to ask about XYZ' consider a separate appointment. Because part of the issue is scarcity of time. So, if a pediatrician has the ability to sit and help you navigate resources, like nutritionists or social workers, that can be deeply helpful." It's freeing not to feel constrained by that brief window during the appointment; you can book an appointment just to discuss navigation to other services and referrals. It's brilliant, right? You're welcome!

Seek Academic Support for School-Aged Kids, from Tweens to Teens and Young Adults

I went from a brisk walk to a light run on my way up the stairs to my son's classroom, as I was already one minute away from the parent–teacher meeting. I really don't like to be late, but I made it right at the hour and my son's teacher greeted me with a smile, "Thanks, Leslie, I'm so glad you could come in. Your son's a great kid but I've noticed that it's really hard for him to remember any details about what he's read or learned in class. He's also struggling to pay attention. Is that happening at home, too?"

I thought about bath time just the night before. "Honey, can you please turn off the bathwater? Did you turn off the bathtub yet?" I was almost used to the frantic refrain, repeating directions over and over again, to get my son to do just about anything. I sighed and admitted, "Yes, it's very consistent with how things go at home. My husband has ADHD so, although he hasn't been diagnosed, we've always known it was a possibility for our kids."

I realize how fortunate I am that that my son's fourth-grade teacher was so attentive because that conversation kicked off a series of calls and Google searches. Although I reached out to schedule a pediatric neurologist within a day of that conversation with his teacher, it took nine months before we could see one. The pandemic hit shortly after that, which interrupted everything, and I spent another 18 months waiting to have neuro-psych tests done that would ultimately confirm my son's diagnosis. Many of us are struggling with how to best support our kids and make sure they are learning, growing, and able to reach their highest potential. This type of guidance often means navigating complex systems, because it's where their academics and health intersect. So, it's often more involved than just dealing with the school system and it takes a *lot* of time, energy, and, depending on your health insurance and what is covered by your school system, money.

How independent are your school-aged kids? If they have medical conditions that affect their needs, there are a whole host of services designed to help get them over the finish line academically speaking. In addition to local coaches, tutors, and after-school academic resources, online services like Wyzant[13] have blossomed to make it easier to find tutors on anything from algebra to French. It's not the main focus of this book and the resource list will continue to evolve but if you do a quick search for "best online tutors for kids" you will find a very long list of options.

Notes

1. https://www.nytimes.com/2018/05/16/upshot/same-sex-couples-divide-chores-much-more-evenly-until-they-become-parents.html#:~:text=By%20Claire%20Cain%20Miller,built%20for%20single%2Dearner%20families
2. https://www.apa.org/pubs/journals/features/sgd-sgd0000109.pdf
3. https://link.springer.com/article/10.1023/B:JADE.0000035626.90331.47
4. https://www.researchgate.net/publication/226158244_Money_Housework_Sex_and_Conflict_Same-Sex_Couples_in_Civil_Unions_Those_Not_in_Civil_Unions_and_Heterosexual_Married_Siblings

5. https://www.tandfonline.com/doi/full/10.1080/10894160.2016.1142350?scroll=top&needAccess=true
6. https://www.biblestudytools.com/dictionary/barabbas/
7. https://momshierarchyofneeds.com/is-good-childcare-the-answer-to-better-mental-health/
8. https://pubmed.ncbi.nlm.nih.gov/25418222/#:~:text=Women%20in%20the%20United%20States,broader%20health%20and%20social%20goals
9. https://patients.amwell.com/
10. https://www.teladochealth.com/
11. https://www.mavenclinic.com/
12. https://wp.me/p8qf85-47h
13. https://www.wyzant.com/

Chapter 7

Outsource or Spouse Source

"Daddy, let's do the Easter eggs!" The kids were asking my husband, relentlessly through Easter weekend, to get started. I delegated the ritual of egg making and decorating to him that year, because not only was it something he would enjoy but I was also completely overloaded in my professional life. The kids were three and seven at the time and it's the type of project where they need both presence and oversight. It's the type of activity I used to like, too, but when you're desperate to reduce your workload, it's like trying to sail in a boat with too much cargo. No matter how much you love "everything" you have to throw things over the side to save yourself. So, my husband bought egg-dyeing equipment in advance, including this fancy egg holder that would allow you to rotate the egg and create designs at the same time. Of course, this felt like overkill to me since every other year we did the eggs old-school. Which means paintbrushes and teacups filled with food dye.

    I gave my husband suggestions on when to start the project. Yes, I was managing the mental load for this endeavor when it got closer to the holiday, even though I delegated it. It takes a good amount of time and a lot of kitchen space. Space that I would also need to make rolls, marinate lamb, mandoline-slice the potatoes, and build a layer cake. I know what you're thinking right now, but the food is always my favorite part of any holiday, so that's where I put the energy. Even if our home is not tidy and the table has mismatched glasses and napkins on it, the food is going to be *fire*! I tried to allow myself freedom from the other details, especially since we weren't having any guests. But I kept returning, unconsciously, to this egg-dyeing project because if my husband and I weren't in sync about the timing, it would just slow down the cooking and baking.

He didn't start the project at all over the Easter weekend, which felt like a win to me because the kids forgot about it and were delighted with all of the other preparations to make the holiday special: their basket hunt, chocolate eggs, and freshly made rolls. So when I came home rushing to get dinner started a few days later, I was floored to find my husband and kids making the Easter eggs. There were cups and bowls with food dye everywhere and eggs in various stages of artistic design drying on the counters.

I was furious. I won't tell you about the conversation (okay, massive argument) we had about it, but more than half of my mental load then (and now) was trying to prevent more unplanned work from falling onto my overflowing plate. There was a time when I really liked to control my environment including how the Easter eggs might look. But that ship sailed shortly after my daughter was born. Micromanaging now, or trying to, meant that the project with the eggs and cleanup would happen at a time that would not interfere with my cooking or cost me 45 precious minutes when I couldn't afford to give it. Of course, this is why many of us "hold" that mental load, and what will work for you depends a lot on your partner's style and capacity. Remember how I mentioned to my son's teacher that my husband has ADHD? Well, I've experimented with a lot of ways to set him up for success with household activities or "reminders" for him to do things where I'm not the one doing the reminding, like using shared notes on the Notes App of my iPhone and to automate reminders, or by inviting him to a "meeting" with a reminder series preset on the calendar, for example, one day before the doctor's appointment, two hours before the doctor's appointment, and then 30 minutes before the doctor's appointment. It's imperfect, because the reality is my husband is impulsive and just doesn't think this way about planning ahead for a project like the Easter eggs or even doctor's visits. If that is your situation, I'd recommend sitting down with your partner and aligning on what type of system works for them in other contexts to plan ahead. For example, there may be something from their professional lives (if that is where they are more organized) that can be used at home. If that doesn't work, the answer might be not to delegate or spouse source multistep projects that intersect with your workload or are prone for misalignment and choose different categories. Or as I share in the next section, working with an expert, like a couples therapist or relationship coach, is another way to make in-home collaboration more effective.

Revisit Norms and Responsibilities with Your Partner

Okay, not everyone has a partner or spouse and even if you do have one, your spouse may not have the mental or physical health to be hands-on with your home or children. Your spouse or partner, again if you have one, also may not have capacity for any number of reasons. So, as you might have guessed from these stories I haven't been nearly as effective at spouse sourcing as I would like to be. When I got married almost 20 years ago, I was overconfident and the implied promise I made then to my now husband was "hey, I'll take over the logistics of your life, our lives together, and when we start a family, I'll do all of the heavy lifting." Now, I was naive and arrogant about what it would take to run a household that included kids. My parents' roles and responsibilities growing up were mostly split along the gendered lines: my dad mowed the lawn and handled finances while my mother oversaw cleaning, meals, and childcare during my earliest memories. But when things were financially very difficult, my father was an active part of mum's housecleaning business and was hands-on cleaning and caring for our space, not just the lawn and car washing by then. My mother was (and still is) an amazing mother so, at some level I wanted to emulate how in charge she was of everything that had to do with childcare. But over 20 years ago, I also could observe how my then boyfriend now husband was pretty disengaged from anything that had to do with cleaning or upkeep in his own apartment, long before we lived together. He's also not neurotypical and his style, among other things, is way more absent-minded professor-like than meticulous. I'm not making excuses for his lack of involvement now; I actively work on it but I'm being very open with you about the fact that like many of us, although I was very planful about a lot of things in my career that mostly came to fruition, I wasn't nearly as thoughtful about how I'd share the household with my now partner.

I'm still living with the aftermath of how I set things up. I never needed a lot of sleep pre-kids. I was nicknamed *the energizer bunny* because I could consistently rely on the privilege of being healthy, combined with my sheer persistence, to get the results I wanted most of the time. I thought there was no amount of housework, personal work, or paid work that would undermine my signature vitality. As I'm sure you know, having kids changed all of it. Not just the process of being physically exhausted and hypervigilant about everything I ate and did through pregnancy and the postpartum recovery but also access to my favorite forms of fuel, which back then were a combination of rest, leisure, and entertainment, disappeared almost overnight. I couldn't just go outside and play when I wanted to, dance when I felt like it, see a friend or read a long book cover to cover. I had babies to care for. And what seemed like an inhumane amount of housework—dishes, laundry, envelopes filled with mail, and bills to attend to, not to mention the demands of my career—which were significant. Pretty quicky after my first child was born, I started trying to renegotiate the bad deal I made with my husband: that I would do "everything" associated with the kids and household and he wouldn't have to worry about it.

Long story short, I'm not the author to do justice to the issue of successful spouse sourcing. I've researched it extensively and know it's an integral part of the "answer" if you are partnered to reduce your workload and get hands-on support for all the things. In my home, I've made progress with my partner and even with my children as they are getting older. But I'll admit it's been slow, messy, and complicated.

Get Clear About What's Expected of You

The good news? I have researched this topic and interviewed brilliant authors like Tiffany Dufu, author of *Drop the Ball*, who have shared the household equitably with their partners. I highly recommend her book; she will encourage you to get past the guilt that often stands in the way of changes. And if you are partnered with a man, you will better understand how much of what feels like what we "should" do is a result of gendered norms and expectations. She's open in her book about starting off her motherhood journey with "home control disease," something that the recovering perfectionists among us might relate to. When I interviewed her for Mom's Hierarchy of Needs, she shared advice that I've continued to use and reuse: "Have a conversation with your circle of three or four people who love you and are invested in your happiness, like close friends, a parent, a spouse, or even kids." Tiffany explained, "[Tell them] '*I feel a sense of overwhelm. I want to be a good (mom, friend, wife, daughter) and I feel I'm not because I have all of these responsibilities. Please write down (or tell me) the list of things you need me to do to be a good mom (or friend or wife)'.*"

This is important because expectations of ourselves are usually so much higher than what other people really need or expect from us.

Uplevel How You Run Your Home

This doesn't mean you need to do more. This means you need to treat it like the sophisticated, multi-stakeholder operation that it is. My other all-time-favorite book about household sharing is by the incredible Eve Rodsky, author of the books *Fair Play* and *Unicorn Space*. I have had the good fortune to get to know Eve, join her Careforce group of volunteers eager to shift the narrative about childcare, and interview her. *Fair Play* is that hands-on, nitty-gritty operating guide on how to get your partner, especially if your partner is a man, to move beyond the gendered divide in the home and with your kids.

The do-it-yourself approach doesn't work for everyone, and there are many sticky issues that couples run into and find difficult to remove themselves from. So, if trying to work through these issues after reading about them isn't moving things forward for you and your family quickly enough or with your goodwill intact, there are incredible people doing this work, such as couples' therapists, coaches, and facilitators. Fair Play facilitators, for example, help couples through the very messy process of implementing equity in the home, and more traditional couples' therapists or clinicians tend to dig into understanding and then unlearning deeply rooted patterns of behavior, especially when those patterns originate in childhood.

Yes, You Can Even Spouse Source with an Ex

We know from our Mom's Hierarchy of Needs studies that women who are partnered with men can grow resentful over time when they own the mental, emotional, and physical workloads for the family. It begins to break the promise of what it means to be in a partnership if that was not the expectation going in. Business partnerships need to be equitable and mutually beneficial, and even if we don't say so, emotionally we hold our romantic partnerships to the same standards. After all, the energy, time, and complexity associated with marriage, which is both an emotional and legal construct, are significant.

Although it's not yet the norm for women partnered with men to have equitable sharing of childcare and household responsibilities, it is changing. I hear from dads often (through the research and my corporate work) and men are also subject to the limiting biases that exist for parenting or caregiving in the workplace. Younger fathers (i.e., under 40) are increasingly more involved in their children's lives and within their households, and according to Pew Research, nearly 20% of stay-at-home parents are dads.[1] More than ever! Pursuing and making progress toward sharing responsibilities in a way that you feel good about is important. Unequal systems eventually fail whether that's a loss of trust, intimacy, connection, happiness, or the relationship itself. So, if you are partnered, and your partnership is safe for you and your kids, it is worth the time, energy, and money if you need additional support like outside counseling to strengthen your relationship and align on mutual expectations.

If you're married or in a committed partnership, you already know it's wonderful and it's hard. Although parenting can deepen the connection with our partners, it also places added strain on our time, energy, and goodwill, so not every couple makes it. Married, two-parent family households, according to the US Census are declining.[2] More children are now raised in single-parent households. Women weren't allowed to own property or get credit without a male cosigner in the United States until the Equal Credit Opportunity Act of 1974,[3] which wasn't all that long ago historically speaking. So in part because women generally have less wealth and in part because we still earn less relative to our male peers, women often end up on the financial losing end of separation and divorce agreements. But there's hope. "You want to try and get the best attorney you can afford." Eve Rodsky, who is also a seasoned estate attorney, explained how the system doesn't favor us. "There are still a lot of unfortunate rules that go all the way back to our relationship with England, including how money and land are passed down. There are terrible assumptions about women. A woman I spoke with was told by her mediator, 'Well, you got to eat bonbons all day for 20 years so, why do you expect your husband to let you sit on your ass now that you're not married?' There was absolutely zero respect for unpaid labor or that she raised his three children while he worked long hours at a law firm."

The Divorce Outcomes for Moms Are Uneven

Eve explained to me that because the system of family law doesn't recognize or value unpaid labor, outcomes for women are still uneven, "There are different health outcomes for women, including a lot of stress and lack of financial support. The words I've heard the most that have taken me aback have been *surprise* and *unexpected*, two words I hate as someone who works in systems. I want to hear *expectations*, I want *knowledge* and *trust*, the opposite of surprise. So, it's important to understand these women felt so taken aback by how the system treated them and their work. Most of the divorced women we've been interviewing recently stated they would have done at least one thing different."

Start Getting More Support with the Written Word

I explained to Eve that this section of the book is about finding those "hidden sources of support that no one talks about" and I knew she'd have an important perspective for single moms and how they can still get more equitable outcomes, even with an ex-partner. Eve said, "We talk about asking for help but we actually don't talk about words enough and I believe that words, whether it's a full contract or it's just snippets of expectations that you write down or email, the written word is a source of support for women because the opposite of the written word is to 'figure it out', which means going to the default systems that don't benefit women."

Eve began her journey to develop the Fair Play method after approaching her husband with a massive "the shit I do" spreadsheet to seek more equitable sharing of the household. You can formally or informally document your efforts and needs. She explained, "If you're getting to a point of resentment in your partnership, or you're going to take a career pause, which often can lead to a divorce or separation, get those expectations down in writing. Spend that time in advance so that you don't have to get to the opposite ends of being caught in these unfair systems. Neha Ruch of The Power Pause and I put together a post-nup [post-nuptial, as in you're already married] document, with questions you can ask."

The post-nup document, developed by Fair Play and The Power Pause (which you can access along with the other resources I mentioned in the Afterword) is designed to support parents who take career pauses to focus on family. Eve said,

> "I love the written word, so it should be documented in some way and doesn't have to look as intense and scary as . . . an actual contract drafted up by a lawyer. The goal is to align expectations, which really includes

what's going to happen to me mentally, emotionally, and financially in this big change? We have some basic questions like if things are changing, how do we want them to change? For example, if I'm taking a step back from my career to support your career, is that going to change the way you view me? What do you think about unpaid labor? Do you think it's valuable or are you going to say that I've just become a housewife down the line? If something happens to your career earning potential what happens to me?"

Although primarily designed to support mothers taking career pauses, many of the questions especially in the "household organization" section of the post-nup document help you align and place monetary value on unpaid labor in the home. This applies whether you plan to pause or not. As I shared previously, because women still pay the "motherhood penalty" in our earnings we are better served creating visibility for this discrepancy. If you've been the person to downshift or pause professionally within your partnership, remember that the often-invisible infrastructure at home enables career success. For example, in the document they recommend a checklist for your post-nup agreement in the absence of a pre-nup (pre-nuptial agreements that outline the financial impact of a separation before marriage) to get really aligned about expectations and shared commitments to the family.

Here's a quick recap of key elements of a post-nup, again from the resource shared by the Fair Play Institute and The Power Pause:

- Written discussion about family goals and financial goals
- Short-term and long-term alignment on the value of the work of the at-home parent (this can be a 50/50 split of

your partner's salary or a combination of the money you're saving because you aren't paying for full-time childcare, house management, etc.)
- Clear financial plan in the partnership (merged bank accounts, retirement funds, etc.)
- A list of financial assets and a mutual understanding of whose name they are under (home, car, etc.)
- A schedule of money meetings to review the budget and check in on how each partner is feeling
- Details on handling debts, responsibilities, assets, and inheritances in the case of a separation

Okay, let's admit: clarity is a beautiful thing, as Eve explained, and the obscurity under which most of us operate in the home can leave us financially and emotionally vulnerable.

If You Go Through a Divorce, Fight for What You and Your Children Deserve

Eve explained,

> "A lot of people try to go to mediation or do a conscious uncoupling, but I've never seen that really work very well. There's the financial component, emotional component, and the caregiving component, and they're all obviously intertwined. But the biggest mistake women make, often because they want to close this chapter of their lives quickly, is that they leave material financial gain on the table. In most cases it makes sense to fight for what's yours and typically that will involve an attorney and some version of a forensic accountant. And what you're fighting for is whatever maximum is allowed under your state law."

Yes, this includes money and resources that have monetary value to honor your values and ease strain on you and your children. She explained,

> "There are many things that women will leave on the table, like pension accounts, IRAs, and, if they have taken a career detour, Social Security. The other thing that makes me really upset is they leave a lot of monetary ambiguity for things that really aren't ambiguous. So, I'll give you an example . . . many will not add into their divorce agreement paying for private school and then all of a sudden, they're scrambling to get their child into a public school the next year, when their child has been going to the same school forever. The courts are not great at helping you make those values assessments, so you want to do that while you're in the fight and the other person wants you to also wrap this up."

According to the Holmes–Rahe Life Stress Scale,[4] which ranks life's most stressful events, divorce and/or separation are at the top, as numbers two and three, respectively. So, if you're going through a separation or divorce, please take care of yourself. We're going to spend the whole next section of this book focused on about self-care strategies to help you refuel.

Get Financial and Logistical Support

A lot of the invisible work we do as mothers is very informal and guided by societal norms. As we know, it's still real work and you can ask for compensation or an equitable split in a separation or divorce agreement. Eve explained, "There's a Fair Play card called 'informal breaks' like all of those school breaks including summer. So, we will see one person saying, 'They valued summer camp for the first 10 years of our marriage, now that our children are 10 and 12, all of a sudden, they're saying they can just ride their bikes all day and won't pay for summer camp'. So, that can put you in a really bad financial situation because you're paying for two to three months of childcare and activities." It's the cost but as Eve and I discussed, there's also the planning time, research, registrations, and driving or commuting to and from each activity to factor in.

She said, "Another Fair Play card is called 'informal education', like teaching your child to ski or any other activities that you'd want to pay for. Another that isn't thought about is after-school activities, whether or not you want your child to engage in those activities, and who's paying for those activities. Spirituality, are you going to be paying for a baptism or membership at a church, synagogue, or mosque."

I've interviewed Eve in the past, after reading *Fair Play*, where she breaks down beautifully the "conception, planning, and execution" steps for over 100 typical household activities. So, whether you make your own list or look at the Fair Play framework, determine what has a monetary component and how it will be paid for.

Don't Forget to Get Help for Emotional Support

Remember the not asking for help part? It's rampant among moms. We love providing support but generally feel awkward about needing it. If you're going through a divorce or separation, or any major life transition really, relying on the people in your life and getting help in every possible way is critical. Eve said, "Because there's often a lot of shame and other social dynamics, like loss of mutual friendships, it's extra lonely to go through a divorce. And in America, admitting that something is a failure, especially your marriage, is very painful. Which often means that they're going to go deeper and darker into the hole. So, because there is such risk to be not supported, this is an area where even just calling out that there are factors conspiring against you to not be supported, you have to legitimately open your mouth and ask for help."

If Possible, Outsource to Paid Support

"Is everything okay?" I asked, half asleep. "No, Les," my sister said. I got a call from my sister explaining that mum said our dad "couldn't talk" and she was on her way to the hospital. Two hours after that, I spoke with her again, along with my father's doctor who explained how serious his stroke was. About five hours later I was at the airport. My father held on for a miraculous four days and I was fortunate to be at his bedside when he passed. My parents recently celebrated their 56th wedding anniversary, and I know how incredibly lucky I am to have had both of my parents cheering me on through life's many plot twists. Even though I knew it could change at any time, I didn't really expect it to. I'm thinking about the lessons and the blessings during this time, and I'm grateful I could drop everything and get on an airplane and leave, with a one-way ticket to Florida without hesitation. I was there for an entire week and until this trip, I'd never been away from my kids for more than two or three nights. I'm fortunate my husband can care for our children, we also have an amazing nanny, and in the spirit of keeping it real, if I didn't have this set up I would have been even more stressed out during this difficult time away. After my father passed away, I stayed for a few more days to spend more time with my sister and my mother. My husband also works full-time, tends to work a very unpredictable schedule, and for several months has been working on an intense project alongside people in several different time zones. He's never been "on point" for the primary household and childcare activities—I won't pretend that I have that fully equal partner yet—but if suddenly, during the crisis situation with my dad, if I had to figure out how to distill everything that needed to be done while I was away and line up other people to support getting the kids to and from their various commitments and doctors' visits while he was at work, it would have been even messier, and it was already messy.

When I was pregnant with my first, after touring a couple of daycares and diving into research about childcare options, I decided to hire a nanny to come to our home. There were a lot of reasons for this, although I didn't know about "mental load" at the time (please see the Table 6.1 in Chapter 6 with childcare options by mental load intensity), the idea of having less complexity, with someone coming to our home versus packing up my son for a commute every day, was very appealing. Ultimately, the deciding factor was that my husband and I both work long and unpredictable hours. Although since then, I have made many changes to my career to accommodate motherhood, I decided early on that I wasn't going to pause or drastically change my career. When my children were babies, I was in roles that involved a lot of travel. During those longer trips, if it was more than a few days, like California or the overseas trips to China, the kids came with me, and sometimes my husband and/or my mom also came with me. But I also was blessed to have the coverage at home I needed if I needed to fly out at 6 a.m. Our nanny at the time would often stay late especially if my husband was in the office, and I was stuck on a runway somewhere for a stalled or delayed flight. It's been an important part of the life support system that enables my work and home life to coexist. While I am gone, she's there managing lunches, pickup, snacks, groceries, laundry, and dishes.

I realize that not everyone can afford, find, or even consider a nanny, and not just because of the cost, which is significant. But if you can afford it and it works for your situation, it's a worthwhile investment to reduce mental load and strain from an uneven household dynamic. Remember in male–female partnerships most of those dad senior leaders have partners at home who are doing all the things, whether they are in the paid workforce or not. So, if you're choosing a path of career growth, or even just preventative health for your own well-being, you will need multiple layers of support behind the scenes. I've spoken with, interviewed, and heard from thousands of moms about this via surveys, and there isn't "one right answer" to the challenge of having too much to do. There are many (many) ways to outsource effectively and not just in ways that cost tons of money.

In this chapter I've also given several examples of spouse sourcing—basically, if "it" has to do with your kids, or your home, and you are partnered (or have a co-parent) that person should be your go-to first port of call for the many requests that are the hardest if not impossible to outsource, such as doctors' visits, parent–teacher meetings, or caregiving through illness, because often, they require parental authority or judgment and occur both frequently and unpredictably.

However, not everyone has access to a healthy, cooperative, or capable spouse. You can find resources—paid and unpaid—in your personal and professional life to reduce the strain of having a list of responsibilities that aren't feasible to tackle. Because remember what we talked about in Section One? The bad feelings, the stress, the mental load, and the decision fatigue all come down to time famine! And time famine is there because you are, like most of us, overworked. Being overworked means you need to be less worked, as in lowering your workload in addition to thinking about your priorities and needs differently.

This is a system! Collectively we are a community of brilliant mothers (and parents) who care and do so much to make this world a better place for ourselves and our families. But to do so, you have to actively involve yourself in the reduction of your workload. Yes, I know it's still "work" to think about how to remove things from your overflowing plate, just like hiring a new employee in your professional life. But the goal is to do very leveraged work and critical thinking that changes how you handle your daily or weekly needs and responsibilities in a sustainable way.

Household Managers or Family Assistants Are an Option

Why, yes, household managers exist. They are not nannies or cleaners or even housekeepers, but people who are in the business of project managing and doing some of those never-ending responsibilities for you. Think of them as dot-connectors taking that mental load away. Appealing right? In 2019, when I interviewed CEO and author of *The Beauty of Success*, Kendra Bracken-Ferguson said, "We had an amazing nanny and made a pact that when my daughter went to preschool, she would go to nursing school. We tried another nanny, and she was just overloaded with walking the dog, running errands, etc. I still needed someone and tried to figure out what I really needed. I went from a full-time nanny to a family assistant, someone who can help coordinate the dog walker, schedule my daughter's appointments, and handle pickup and drop-off." During that interview was the first time I had heard about this type of alternate role. Whether you look for a "family assistant" or "household manager," there are options to carve out part-time or fractional support in ways that optimize your time.

The idea to hire a household manager came to Kelly Hubbell, who later founded My Sage Haus, when she was pregnant with her third child and feeling overloaded by the amount of household management. She explained,

> "Raising a family is almost like scaling a business. When you add more people to our household, just like when you add more people to a business, you need to set yourself up with better systems and

operations for the household to function. Things were starting to really fall through the cracks and I decided we needed to divide the labor more equitability. With my husband starting a business and me taking on a lot of the household tasks in addition to my full-time job, I was feeling overwhelmed. So, I made a long list of all the things I was doing to support our household and took it to my husband, and he looked at it and said, 'this looks like a job description' and I was like, 'Oh, because it is a job.' That's when I realized, although I'm doing this, it's a role, and what if we found somebody to help us fulfill a lot of the tasks and responsibilities to help run our family?"

Household managers, as I discussed with Kelly, are not just for celebrities. If you're not at a stage where you need or want to hire a nanny or have responsibilities that fall outside of a typical housekeeper role, you can hire someone into this more flexible, part-time, or even fractional position. Kelly said, "The first step is making the invisible labor visible and then to decide, 'okay, what is my budget? How do I make this a reality for myself?' In thinking about my family's needs, in addition to what can I afford, then it's thinking about 'how am I prioritizing my life right now?' Most of us have to really prioritize how we could potentially fit it in and what is the value we put on a lot of this cognitive invisible labor in our home?"

Kelly researched comparable positions in her local area, like the costs for housekeepers, eldercare givers, and nannies, to get a sense of what would be a realistic job spec and compensation rate. She added, "It is a very diverse role. You need someone super versatile. So, I thought if we can afford $200 a week, that's about eight hours backing into our budget at an hourly rate. Then I went back to my spreadsheet because I put a time allocation next to every task and kept sorting it until I figured out what are some of the tasks that could fill up that eight hours that I would love to off-load. The next step was then creating a job description and putting it out on different platforms to start recruiting to find the right fit. "What's better than finding and hiring that perfect household manager? Well, it's finding someone who can do that for you." Seriously, Kelly now does this in her business. But as you think about your needs, the sky is the limit on your wildest dreams and aspirations. There are service-based solutions for just about every common challenge we face now and there's no glory in going down with the overwhelmed ship. If you can afford it, do it. The "mom job" is impossibly big, not the love part, but the logistics and scope. Think for a moment about all of the responsibilities in the bottom two-thirds of the Mom's Hierarchy of Needs framework, like the household responsibilities, our professional roles, and/or community commitments, and, of course, children's well-being and milestones. And outsourcing, whether it's a household manager, nanny, or house cleaner or keeper is about much more than having less on your to-do list. As Kelly shared, "Hiring a household manager was absolutely transformative to my life, happiness, productivity, and ability to be present with my kids. I could also better empathize with and understand my partner. It wasn't just about 'I got back an hour today because I didn't check the pantry list, go to the store, and unload the groceries.' I no longer was holding space in my mind for all of those things."

Okay so getting support is everything and there are many ways that you can begin to get the help and resources you need. Once your workload is lighter, you can free up mental, physical, and calendar space to do more of what fuels you. As we'll cover in the next section, finding those critical sources of fuel is key to living that full, healthy life you deserve.

A Little Review of How to Ease Your Workload

So, we covered a lot of territory in this chapter about ways to ease your workload. My hope is that you emerge feeling inspired and optimistic. Always, there's something that can be shifted to make things better. Before we move onto Section Three—all about refueling—here's a quick recap on the key tools you can use to begin:

- Get really clear about what you want to spend your time on.

    This includes thinking about your current goals and highest priorities, with a focus on no more than three during any given season. Make your seasons quarterly instead of drifting into the "set it and forget it" energy. Your kids keep changing so your support systems need to change frequently, too.

- Become laser focused on trimming your to-do list at home.

    No judgment here; you can choose what's on your list of "not-to-do" things for any number of reasons. A fabulous mom founder told me, "She is not interested in sending thank-you cards and if people in her family expect them, they should not give them gifts." I request (okay, insist) that my kids have fruit or vegetables with every meal. After years of simmering frozen peas to cook them for their lunch on the weekends, my son informed me that he likes the peas cold. As in, frozen. So, I inquired how my daughter felt and she also preferred the "fun, popsicle like" peas. That was my signal to stop taking that extra step to cook them when I pull their weekend lunch together.

    Some people don't want to peel fruit, pack lunches, match socks, dye their hair, or wear makeup anymore. Although I've included a few options for your consideration on how to determine what's not connected to your priorities, outside of your areas of strength, or that you've

outgrown (metaphorically speaking) in some other way, you get to decide.
- Reassess and renegotiate on your to-do list in your professional life.

   If it's in your personal life, your options are to outsource, spouse source, eliminate from the list altogether, or potentially, if age appropriate, upskill your kids. Does it matter if socks are rolled perfectly? If it's in your career and delegation isn't an option, have a candid but thoughtful conversation with your manager or stakeholders about how to reassess deadlines and resources to ensure projects are delivered in high quality but without burning you or the rest of the team out. There's also a systems guide referenced for you in the Afterword all about this with examples.
- Know that boundary setting doesn't always work. For example, if you lack psychological safety in the workplace, set boundaries with a group ask instead of an individual ask. Either use your employee resource group for parents and caregivers or if you don't have one, collaborate with colleagues who have similar needs. For example, "we think that meetings should not be scheduled after 4 p.m., because it conflicts with many of the parents' pick-up times."

   If you understand when you are most likely to betray your own needs or interests (i.e., your boundary triggers), then create a script that you can refer to (in your notes on your phone or a document where you can either recite a variation of it when you need to or you can copy and paste it into an email).

   For example, "I can't join the volunteer event next Saturday. Thank you for thinking of me but I prioritize weekends as family time and it's particularly challenging to get childcare coverage then."
- Review your childcare options (and needs) regularly as your kids grow.

Factor in not only hard costs and availability but also time and mental energy to manage and maintain the arrangement. Consider tapping into nontraditional childcare resources for back up, after-school, and occasional needs; there are hidden options that may help you.

Notes

1. https://www.pewresearch.org/short-reads/2023/08/03/almost-1-in-5-stay-at-home-parents-in-the-us-are-dads/
2. https://www2.census.gov/library/publications/2024/demo/p20-587.pdf
3. https://womenshistory.si.edu/blog/voices-independence-four-oral-histories-about-building-womens-economic-power#:~:text=As%20a%20result%20of%20her,on%20sex%20or%20marital%20status
4. https://www.stress.org/wp-content/uploads/2024/02/Holmes-Rahe-Stress-inventory.pdf

Section Three

FUEL YOUR FUTURE

Chapter 8

Why Health Span Matters to Your Potential

"**D**id it hurt more *while* you were running?" she asked. I hesitated before responding. "It was hurting more when I went running, yes, but I stopped and slowed down to a walk for the last half a mile or so. Could it just be from my vaccines?" I asked hopefully.

I tried to explain (again) to the nurse that I had the COVID vaccine along with the shingles vaccine the day before, which I now realize was probably way too much vaccination for my body at the same time. I felt crappy from the time I woke up to the time I dragged myself through the streets for a shorter-than-usual run.

"You need to go to the emergency room, Leslie. We can't evaluate you properly here, and the pain you're experiencing could be a heart attack. We'll let them know that you're coming, but please go there now."

I was not surprised by this, because it had happened before when I had similar pain in my chest; however, this time I was pretty convinced I was feeling the ill effects of the double vaccination. Despite this, the nurse wouldn't budge.

After I checked in at the emergency room, I spent 12 hours there. They were so busy that I was seen in a hallway. I spent most of that night masked up, working on my article for the week in a crowded waiting room. Typing away, tuning out the noise from announcements and other patients, I comforted myself by tucking into the productivity zone—the place I love to go the most, straight past worry right to the corner of "getting things done" and clarity.

I was lucky, I was fine. Later that week, I told my doctor that the next time they asked me to go to the ER I would need to have a hatchet in my head, a joke that I made in poor taste, but she laughed anyway. I knew that they would send me, and I also knew that it was the right decision, based on the symptoms I had and my family history. My mother had a mild heart attack shortly before my son was born, and due to the family history on my father's side, they were being understandably cautious. It wasn't just because of me and my high blood pressure, but all of the surrounding indicators that point to elevated risk.

As I shared in Chapter 1, women in general are at greater risk for stress-related illness. Women live nine less healthy years than men, and when we have heart disease, it's more likely to be fatal. And Black women are at 60% greater risk for fatal heart disease.

While we run those extra loads of laundry, obsess over the slightest changes in our children's health or educational needs, plot out narrow intersections of availability between meetings, games, performances, appointments, and deadlines we continue to rack up the mental calories, draw from our physical reserves and place additional fragmentation in the form of constant interruptions from "starting and stopping" into our lives. Although there's probably no medical study that defines exactly what that "stress" tipping point looks like for each person, we do know from research and studies that chronic stress makes us physically ill.

Health Span Equals More Well-Being

We've all read those cute ages and stages guides for our kids, providing assurance that the "right" nutrition, sleep, vaccination protection, cognitive stimulation, and developmentally appropriate activities are achievable based on what's happening to their minds and bodies as they grow. However, as we age the rules are murkier. We all know about the basics (like sleep, movement, and hydration) that apply to everyone. But more specific guidance is possible based on your individual health history and life stage. Although it's still not the experience many of us have during our annual checkups, innovation is happening behind the scenes in the medical field, including more precise "personalized medicine" often in the form of functional or holistic medical practices and the growing body of research about women's health needs.

Throughout your journey, you need to pay attention to everything at the top of the Mom's Hierarchy of Needs framework to some degree and not just the things you expect, like stress management, sleep, movement, and adequate nutrition. Those are important but we also need include things in the very top category and lower top third that may not be on your radar, like maintaining healthy adult relationships, fun, interests, learning, and development. I will put in a plug here for my wellness app, on the Mom's Hierarchy of Needs website (timecheck.momshierarchyofneeds.com), where you can track your time either weekly or daily and see what the recommended guidance is. For example, we hear a lot about sleep, which is typically seven to nine hours for an adult, but we don't hear as much about time spent learning. You always have discretion over what works for you but having a joyful mix of self-care activities beyond sleep and exercise makes it a bit less challenging.

Many of us enjoyed the thoughtful recommendations about "what to do" during pregnancy and the postpartum window. But what about everything you need after that? Right, there aren't a whole lot of health guides helping us proactively manage our well-being over the long haul.

Health span has been a quiet, growing movement mostly among people who are either super interested in their health because it's tied to their livelihoods, like athletes, or those who have more discretionary income and time. When I stumbled on influencers in the health span space in 2016, it was before I started Mom's Hierarchy of Needs or worked for companies where I interviewed doctors, researchers, and experts. What intrigued me was that they weren't just talking about longevity and doing the things we need to extend our lives. They were talking about more healthy years, where we can enjoy a higher quality of engagement with the types of things we love and sometimes assume we'll have access to forever. I mean, who doesn't want more healthy years? Right. Let's go get it!

In Dr. Peter Attia's book, *Outlive: The Science and Art of Longevity*, he suggests choosing a short list of what you'd want to be able to do when you're 100 years old, what he calls the *centenarian decathlon*, but instead of running over high jumps or lifting 100-pound weights, he explains it's the everyday things we find useful, like being able to bring groceries up a flight of stairs, pull a suitcase down from the overhead bin on an airplane, or pick up a grandchild—all activities that people have a hard time doing unless they've put focus in their forties and fifties on strength and endurance. Training for health span is more intense than training for longevity. I won't go into the details of that here because it's well documented in his book and others and frankly, the detail of it can become daunting.

What I want you to know is that this health span movement is here, it's useful, and it's something we all need access to. But a lot of moms are too busy cleaning counters or researching summer camps to opt in. Remember when I said health for moms is my ministry? Well, the why behind this book is that we must, must, must opt in! Yes, it's lovely to be healthy and happy for our children and future grandchildren, our partners, and even our friends, but more than anything this movement is for us. Let's remain faithful to optimization, not only for errands or our careers but also time with good health.

Even if you don't know what your VO2 max is (the maximum amount of oxygen you can use while exercising), you can work on getting in more aerobic fitness, like walking, dancing, or jumping with your kids in the living room. If you wear a smart watch (or other wearable device that tracks your exercise), you may have a decent estimate of your VO2 max already, I was surprised to find mine within my Apple Health data and was delighted to see how good it is. So, some of us are training at intense levels but you don't need to go fully into health span hyperdrive because starting at full speed will probably feel a bit like chaperoning a class full of kindergarteners for the first time: overwhelming at best and demotivating at worst.

I've tried to summarize mom-friendly approaches and provide you with a health span entry ramp. You can get onto the health span highway with healthier behaviors and stay there, before potentially graduating to more intense training activities. The reality is, better is better and a good way to think about any lifestyle changes. We all know the problem with wellness for most mothers isn't a lack of willpower, it's a lack of discretionary time. I'm surprised, however, how few mothers I speak with understand what's at stake for our health and how the biological and logistical cards are stacked against us in ways that threaten our longevity.

Start to Personalize Your Approach to Well-Being

When people ask you, "how are you doing?" you probably say, "fine" or "well" most of the time. Wellness includes your state of mind and perspective on how things are going, but there are many other more objective measures of your overall well-being you can take advantage of. We are not a "one-size-fits-all" community as moms, but we are a community, and I want anyone who is in a greater risk group to pay extra attention to that. Sometimes that might have to do with what runs in your family, which is true for me as well, or it could be your race, ethnicity, or cultural background. Ask your doctor point blank if you are in a higher risk category for certain things and, if so, what are the proactive steps, screenings, or tests you can take now.

We're pretty busy with our kids, homes, careers, and communities, so we routinely deprioritize our own health, but you have to resist that. Whether it's your race or ethnicity, LGBTQ+ status, disabilities, family history, or cultural background, view your health through that prism of intersecting light to personalize your approach and needs. Start with tapping the health experts in your midst by asking your practitioners for their guidance on what you should do or have checked and how frequently.

Organize Your Care Team

"You should not have done that, Leslie! That's ridiculous!" my husband, clearly upset, felt that I had crossed a line. "But . . . look, I didn't hear back from you right away and the health sharing app said your heart rate was elevated but you hadn't been moving. Sounds serious to me. Why wouldn't you check with your doctor?" So, this argument was because I overused my "directly contact my partner's doctor" privileges by sending screenshots from my husband's health data and the recent warnings that came to me about his heart rate. Thankfully, his primary care doctor didn't think it was a concern, but I was able to schedule him to go in shortly after.

My husband is, shall we say, anti-exercise and despite all of the things I learn about and do to extend health span, I've had very little influence on my husband's behavior. At least, not yet. In fairness though, there have been times where I haven't wanted to go in to see my own doctor or check on my own illnesses because I've felt "too busy" to address them, and my husband has pushed me to make sure that I'm seen. Sometimes you can have that type of accountability with your partner, if you have one, or even with a friend or close family member, to make sure that if something comes up you're not second-guessing whether or not to address it with an expert.

Begin at the beginning. Regardless of where you are on your health journey, tap into the experts you already have access to and build a strong, trusted care team. What does that look like? Assemble the right people and see them with the frequency required to monitor your changing needs and guide you toward further support when necessary. You need to feel seen and heard with your doctors and medical practitioners. If you don't, that alone is a good reason to make changes.

I'm fortunate to live in a community with a lot of great doctors and I'm the "doctor finder" in my family, which includes the kids and my partner. Here are a few key questions you can start with to assess whether you have the right medical practitioners now, when you are considering someone new, or if you want to make changes:

- Do you feel comfortable asking questions, regardless of how detailed or vague they are?
- Is your health care practitioner responsive when you try to reach them?
- Do you have multiple ways of reaching them that are convenient for you (e.g., can you use an email via a secure patient platform in addition to calling their office)?
- When you raise concerns do they listen or dismiss you?

- Are they within a close enough proximity that if you're having a problem, you will go in to see them instead of avoiding a long commute?
- When they tell you they're going to follow up with additional information or appointments, do they honor those commitments? Or do you have unresolved mystery issues within their area of expertise for an extended period of time without a set of next steps?
- Is their training, education, and experience in the area that is relevant for your needs, especially if your needs change?
- If they are not from your cultural, ethnic, or racial background, do they stay current on risk factors that might disproportionately affect your health and well-being?

Stay Proactive with Your Primary Care and Obstetrician–Gynecologist (OB-GYN) Visits

You probably have a primary care doctor or health care provider because it's hard to get insurance to pay for anything without one. How often do you see your obstetrician-gynecologist (OB-GYN)? A lot of us (including me for quite a while) stop seeing our OB-GYNs, because we've found the ideal birth control, are done with having kids, or feel well supported by our other medical practitioners. But these doctors are trained in not only reproductive health and helping you prevent or sustain pregnancies but also helping diagnose, care for, prevent, and navigate a lot of conditions that are specific to women's bodies, like fibroids or endometriosis.

So, if you haven't seen yours in a while, make an appointment. I discovered quite by accident when I reconnected with mine that because I hadn't seen her in over three years, they treated me like a brand-new patient. Why does that matter? Being treated like a brand-new patient means it takes longer to get in for an appointment. In effect they're setting you up once again in their system, which takes more time.

Our health care practices will not necessarily tell us in advance so stay active with appointments to avoid this so please make sure you see your OB-GYN annually.

I had the opportunity to attend a fibroids awareness event hosted by three nonprofits (the White Dress Project, Resilient Sisterhood, and Boston Medical Center), over the summer, which I shared in more detail from an article on Mom's Hierarchy of Needs.[1] During that event, Dr. Yvonne Gomez-Carrion, who has been an OB-GYN for 41 years suggested, "If you're going to a provider for the first time, take a partner. And I don't mean you have to bring a sexual partner.[2] Just someone with another set of ears who can take notes. Because I am from Brooklyn and can talk fast, I encourage my patients to record the visit. And if you're going to a provider who's intimidated by that, that's not the right provider. Because our job is to answer your concerns."

Another fabulous OB-GYN whom I've interviewed in the past, Dr. Lucy Lomas,[3] who is also the executive director of the New England Medical Association, recommends keeping notes about changes to your health on an ongoing basis. Whether that's electronic notes on your phone or a notebook, doesn't matter, but keeping a record enables you to share details that are easy to forget, like frequency and time frames, if you've experienced something.

Many of us also see specialists frequently or occasionally, for example, your mental health care providers or therapist, cardiologist, ophthalmologist or other eye care practitioner, allergist, or ear, nose, and throat (ENT) doctor. Basically, those experts are trained to dive deep on some specific part of your body or a specific health condition. If you need one, when you need one, and whom you need to see, tends to be recommended by your primary care doctor or perhaps even your insurance company. There's a wide range of functional medicine practitioners, including naturopathic doctors, nurse practitioners, physicians' assistants, and medical doctors or primary care practitioners who approach patient care differently. What's exciting about this space is that functional medicine practitioners are rising in popularity, and they tend to focus on what primary care doctors used to have time to do back in the day. They oversee your entire body, including your routines, health, and wellness practices, and discuss your needs, symptoms, supplements, and medications very holistically and proactively. They're not always covered by insurance, but they are in some cases.

Explore Preventative Testing

There are the critical health screenings that we all hear about, such as mammograms, colonoscopies, and skin cancer checks, but functional medicine doctors will likely recommend additional tests to assess your health risks. For example, do you have biomarkers that might indicate greater risk factors for particular illnesses or conditions? For example, I learned about ApoB[4] testing as a more precise predictor of heart disease risk through my research, and because of my mother's history, I asked my primary care doctor to have the tests done during my last physical. She was awesome and didn't hesitate but probably would not have recommended that test for me because I'm an avid exerciser with low cholesterol, but I still wanted to know. Luckily, my results were normal. I realize not everyone wants that more "predictive" information but I'm a planner and maybe you are, too. If so, having time to address lifestyle and behavioral changes that can positively affect your health, versus not having that lead time, seems better. At least to me it does but as always, you get to choose your own adventure.

Your primary care doctor can order many (if not all) of these newer tests. Some people also obtain them from genetic testing sites and place the orders online, but if you are able to access them with your primary care doctor, you can ask questions, receive additional support, and, hopefully, have them covered by your insurance. I walk into my primary care appointments with a list, based on my family's health history and the research I conduct, and it's a great way to spark a conversation with my doctor about monitoring my long-term health needs.

Systematize Your Preventative Care

Have you had an annual physical in the past year? If not, please schedule one immediately, as in, pause this book or put it down. Don't worry, you know I'll be here when you get back. Ditto for your OB-GYN visit. These appointments can be unwieldy to keep track of. At one point, my sister and I were trying to schedule all of the annual visits my parents needed to have, during the month of January. We wanted there to be one time of the year, where all of their preventative health screenings happened and we could plan ahead to have those conversations, make sure both parents were not in Barbados at the time, and join if necessary in person or by phone. Wouldn't it be brilliant to have a "health month" when all of your major checkups—for your heart, uterus, eyes, and anything else that needs to be reviewed annually, get done?

If you can consolidate, then you can submit your reimbursement requests or receipts for health savings accounts if you have them at one time, plan any follow-up activity your doctors may recommend within a common time frame, or otherwise just sit back and bask in the glow of a major task well done until the next year.

I've not been able to do this with the kids because their annual physicals are near their birthdates, and their specialists, in some cases, see them every six months. But I've grouped most for myself now (e.g., eye doctor, primary care doctor) into the beginning of the year and the OB-GYN is in the late summer. Generally, I make the next year's appointment for anything annual right at the time I'm checking out from the doctor's office. Before I leave, I put the new appointment onto my digital calendar in my phone and set a reminder for two weeks before and the second reminder for one day before and the third one, two hours before the appointment. If the appointment is early in the morning or late in the day, when I need to make sure my husband is home with the kids, I'll "invite" him to the calendar invite so he's aware of it.

However, sometimes, the medical practice doesn't have their calendars open that far ahead. If so, I ask when they start scheduling and I put that date, with two reminders, into my calendar as an appointment. I will name it "Schedule with Dr. XYZ" versus "In-person appointment with Dr. XYZ," or for those virtual visits, "Virtual appointment with Dr. XYZ" so it's a bit easier to search for and find digitally. Then the next time you wonder, "did I schedule all of my medical appointments for this year?" you can easily find the full list categorized by month. You're welcome!

Speak with Your Elders (If You Can) and Update Family Health History

If you are fortunate to be able to talk to your older family members about their health and history, take that step, too. Call your parents, aunties, uncles, and second cousins. Many of us, especially those of us from immigrant communities where people do not like to talk about health, may not know such history. So, I will tell you, people from Barbados, at least those who are in the generation of my parents, do not like to go to the doctor, let alone explain in detail some type of malady. Anytime I had to go to see a doctor when I was there, except for the hospital, the waiting rooms were practically empty. So, you might have to overcome some resistance among your crew to get answers, but you can start asking the questions.

Dig Deeper Only If It Interests You

I've spent a lot of time researching health span, fitness, mental health, and some of the latest and greatest advice about supplements, nutrition, and strength training because it's fascinating to me and perhaps because I'm a little bit of a control freak when it comes to my body. My quirks aside, it's wonderful to know about activities that work but it's also a lot. Some of you are thinking . . . bring it! So, if you want to dive deep, perhaps the best comprehensive resource I've read so far is Dr. Peter Attia's book, *Outlive*, which I mentioned, and from a perimenopause/menopause perspective, *Estrogen Matters* by Dr. Avrum Z. Bluming and Dr. Carol Tavris. Please know that *Outlive* is long and both books are quite detailed for a nonmedical person, but if you love research like I do, you will enjoy them.

Notes

1. https://momshierarchyofneeds.com/our-health-needs-are-often-overlooked-how-to-find-the-support-you-deserve/
2. https://momshierarchyofneeds.com/how-to-restore-warmth-and-excitement-to-your-long-term-relationship/
3. https://www.linkedin.com/in/drlucylomas/
4. https://pmc.ncbi.nlm.nih.gov/articles/PMC10488498/#:~:text=They%20found%20that%20using%20apoB,In%202021%2C%20Johannesen%20et%20al

Chapter 9

The Importance of Emotional Health

"Mum, how are you doing?" I was walking to the train because, typically, the daily call to my mother is while I'm in transit.

She responded, "Les, I feel slow."

"Slow? What do you mean by that . . . do you feel sick?"

"No."

"Do you feel sad or down?" I pressed for detail. "Les, I just feel slow." She said it a little more quickly and there was a touch of irritation in her voice. I wanted more precision than *slow*, a word you'd use to describe a racehorse and not your disposition. After we hung up, I immediately called my sister, "Pril, Mum said she's feeling slow again. Is everything okay?"

Shortly before my son was born, my mother had a heart attack, seemingly out of nowhere. Thankfully, my parents lived with my sister at the time, and it was a mild heart attack. Still, it surprised everyone, including her doctors. Why did my then 70-year-old spry mum who walked every day and remained active, who had never smoked in her life, and didn't have more than a glass of wine at a time ever have a heart attack?

Of course, health and health conditions are complicated. In this case, they attributed my mother's sudden heart attack to stress so, you may think well okay she was stressed, and stress is bad for the heart. The end. However, there's another story behind this story. As I've shared throughout the book, my parents were plagued with a series of crises, including financial and legal challenges, since my sister and I were kids. Mum, being who she is, has carried the weight of these emotional storms. She is also a proud Bajan woman, who came to the United States with the American dream of "stability" and "freedom" and attached a lot of shame to the struggles.

We're all going to find ourselves wading in and out of the deep-stress waters throughout the different life circumstances we experience. Without interventions, as I've already shared, the stressors themselves tend to be less important than the accumulation and lack of relief. Have you ever had your dishwasher break down? You know, at some fantastic time like after a party or Thanksgiving dinner? Well, it's the same concept.

Usually, you need at least several days if not an entire week to get someone out to fix it. So, the problem isn't that you had wonderful meals with multiple courses and guests and used more dishes than you usually would. Because you planned for it; after all, it was a celebration! The problem is the broken dishwasher and inability to deal with those dishes plus the new dishes in the days before the repair. That pileup isn't pretty, and stress over time, is the same. The best way to protect your health from the inevitable stressors we have to deal with is to notice when it's becoming a problem.

Managing Through the Spiral of Scarcity Thinking

"When people feel burned out or are on that track, one of the things we see is they develop a scarcity mindset. Like, 'I don't have time to work' or 'I don't have time to take a break' or 'I don't have time to do all of these things!' It can be hard to reason with them," said Dr. Charmain Jackman, clinical psychologist, founder of InnoPsych, and author of *The Black Therapist's Guide to Private Practice and Entrepreneurship*.

Remember scarcity thinking, one of the three ghosts I shared in Section One? Time famine is a very real problem at the heart of everything we struggle with. But if you begin down a path of feeling like "there's just no time" for your health or enjoyment, pay attention. When we resist trying new strategies, receiving support, or the wise counsel to pause, it can be an early warning sign that stress is moving you into the red zone of burnout or worse.

Identify Your Own Unique Stress Tells

Charmain went on to explain,

> "I will often ask patients, 'what does stress look like for you? What does stress feel like in your body?' We all have different signs, and I know that when I have a deadline coming up, I'm going to stay up late to try to power through this. So, I'm going to be cranky with people. Maybe my husband will make a comment about something I'm doing like, 'oh, you came to bed kind of late last night' or I may notice that I'm irritable. I may rush through putting the kids to bed so I can go back and work."

There's a lot of power in understanding your specific signs that you're heading in the wrong direction emotionally. Think about the last few times you were in a bad place: what was your schedule like? How were you treating yourself and others you love? Did you maintain, reduce, or abandon your self-care routines? For example, on a smaller scale, I know that if I start reading the same paragraph over and over again when I'm trying to work, it's a cue I need to get up and take a walk, or if it's at night, go to sleep. Do you know the signs when you've reached a point where you can't function well?

Follow the Breadcrumbs Away from Burnout

Understanding those little clues can lead you to action. If you agree with yourself on what the warning signs mean, you can start to unwind the current state of things, and if you are in or nearing burnout, reset. The word *burnout* gets used a lot now for good reason but it can mean different things to different people. So, I'm going to keep it real: burnout is no joke, despite how prevalent it is, don't minimize it. Each time I've recovered from burnout, it was not fast, so take it seriously and be very patient with and good to yourself at each step. Also, what some people call burnout can really be something more serious, like depression, so you may want to seek expert help in the form of a therapist or begin with a thorough medical checkup with your primary care doctor. In parallel, with the resources I'm about to share in this chapter, please revisit the tools at your disposal for workload relief (in the home and/or your professional life) from Section Two. Ask yourself where you need support and what the fastest path would be to ease added strain?

Sufficient Sleep Is Table Stakes for Your Well-Being

"Leslie, you don't look like you're doing well. Are you okay?" my colleague closed the door to her office, before asking me this question. I slumped down into the chair she offered and tried to explain. She looked genuinely concerned and my response probably came out in a sleep-deprived word jumble.

"My daughter isn't sleeping through the night. As a matter of fact, she's happiest sleeping on a human, not in her crib or the co-sleeper. She rarely sleeps in the stroller and will not sleep in a car like most babies; otherwise, I'd just drive around at night if I needed to. I'm waking up every 90 minutes to feed her and I've started hallucinating. It's brutal."

She listened and validated my experience. "Oh, Leslie, I completely understand. I had terrible issues with sleep. Have you ever considered a night nanny? I had to go that route after my twins were born, and it's pricey, but it was probably the best money I ever spent." At this point, I was working in the childcare and eldercare industry so I had certainly heard the term *night nanny* but hadn't even considered that as an option. I assumed that was something that "other people" like those who also had private jets or drivers might do. But in that moment, speaking with her about her experience, the idea of it became really appealing.

Now, neither of my kids slept through the night until they were 14 months old, despite reading every "how to get your kid to sleep" book, trying and then failing to have the stomach for cry it out, and consulting with a pediatric sleep scientist. Before that, pregnancy both times activated sciatica, which kind of feels like having a toothache in your lower back and upper leg all the time, causing pain day and night and sending me to physical therapy for the last trimester. Through years of trying to conceive, before I even became pregnant, I went through several rounds of in vitro fertilization, with its hormones and crack-of-dawn bloodwork, which also disrupted my sleep. So, basically in the journey to become a mom, there were at least six years where my sleep was inconsistent at best.

I hired a night nanny only once for one night, from the same service that my colleague recommended, because at the time I was also really worried about our finances. But wow, one night of getting nearly five hours of sleep in a row was worth the $250. Bear in mind if this appeals to you, you still have to get up to pump milk if you are breastfeeding, but I felt like a full human again and it helped to shake me out of the terrible spiral I was in. Because sleep is so critical to our reasoning, thinking, memory, and planning, many of my decisions during that time were compromised. I'm so grateful to my former colleague Erica and the friends during that period of my life who cared enough to be candid.

In hindsight, I realize that I could've explored more alternatives and leaned on my partner for additional coverage, although he was providing a fair amount of coverage early in the evening. Wonderful advice my OB-GYN provided was to make sure that I introduced the baby to a bottle within the first couple of weeks so that I could have someone else (e.g., my partner or even my mom while she was staying with us) feed the baby. My husband usually stayed with the baby from the time I went to sleep the first time through one bottle feeding. Typically, this gave me about three hours of sleep in a row, which was great but I could have asked for more. My sister and her husband very kindly stayed up one night when we were in Florida on vacation for the holidays and watched the baby so that my husband and I could have a long-overdue night to ourselves for dinner and several hours of sleep. If your lack of sleep is because your kids don't sleep, and you have a local network with friends, family, or others who love you, sound the alarm and ask for help! Or better still, talk to your doctor or medical practitioner about options.

There Are Many Barriers to Good Sleep

"I dropped her . . . . I can't believe I dropped her!" I was frantically explaining to my husband while handing him our daughter. I adjusted the phone to my other ear while putting on pants in anticipation of a visit to the emergency room. My husband asked, "she looks okay; are you sure?" I said, "she definitely hit her head . . . honey, I'm so sorry, I can't believe it happened. She wriggled out of my arms as I was trying to put her down into her crib and I was so sleepy, it felt like it happened in slow motion." When I reached the on-call doctor from the pediatrician's office, they asked some basic questions as I explained what happened. On the way to the children's hospital, I held my then infant daughter so closely terrified that I had screwed up and damaged her health beyond repair. I was blessed with a perfect, beautiful, clever baby and I was convinced that I ruined it. After about six hours at the hospital, we emerged with a clean bill of health. They said, she was fine but that night and for a long time afterward, I felt like the worst mother on the planet. Right before it happened, I remembered feeling so relieved that I would be able to go to sleep. Again, neither of my kids slept through the night for a too-long while. By the time my daughter was about 10 months old, I was already hallucinating most nights. You may have experienced this, and if so, I'm very sorry. It's like being out of your mind with fatigue. I was dangerously tired; I knew it, too, but I also didn't do anything drastic . . . because it seemed like such a normal new baby experience for parents. I kept waiting for sleep training and other conventional wisdom to set in. But in hindsight, I should have treated my lack of sleep like an emergency long before I lost hold of my baby.

In the most recent wave of the Mom's Hierarchy of Needs post-pandemic study, which began in January 2023 and is still running as I write this in 2025, 64% of moms want to make "more sleep" part of their self-care routine. Exercise is still number one (69% as I write this), "more me time" and "quality time with spouse" are tied for number two (63%), and sleep is currently number three (62%), followed by pursuit of a hobby or interest (59%). Sleep is always in the top three whenever I ask variations on this question, which is not surprising, since countless studies show good-quality sleep is essential for memory, mood, and immune function. If you ask just about any parent "how are you doing?" there is a reasonable chance they will answer with some version of "tired" or "exhausted." So, before you start feeling guilty about not getting enough sleep, on top of everything else you're worried about, know that more than a third of American adults report not getting enough sleep, according to the CDC.[1] So, sleep is a huge, known health problem in our society for everyone, not only parents. For women, there are additional factors, including hormonal changes, that can influence our sleep patterns, especially during the pregnancy, postpartum, or perimenopausal phases.

The best conversation I had to learn more about the nuances affecting our sleep was with Dr. Shelby Harris, licensed psychologist and author of *The Women's Guide to Overcoming Insomnia: Get a Good Night's Sleep Without Relying on Medication*, a book about the sleep challenges women uniquely face. I'm including a few highlights from our discussion, some of which were originally published on Mom's Hierarchy of Needs. She said, "When I think about sleep for women, there are three different circles, kind of like a Venn diagram, that overlap and have insomnia or sleep loss in the center. There are psychological, social, and biological factors."

Rest Is Essential for Good Sleep

There are many unavoidable barriers that come between us and a good night's sleep, including underlying medical conditions that you can have a doctor or health care practitioner assess for. But you may not be aware of that there is one often accessible factor within your control, rest. Shelby said, "Rest and sleep are different. Rest is a period of just quiet, not moving, and quieting the brain. Really, it's experiencing a moment of stillness where your brain is not multitasking but unwinding. Sleep is when you're not having any conscious awareness and that's totally different. There are different stages of sleep that are restorative or repairing for the body and it's different."

She also explained that sleep is an irrepressible need at night versus "non-sleep rest," which helps calm us down and relax our minds.

> "We don't want to go, go, go and then try to crash at night. Make sure you make time to rest during the day because otherwise your brain is not going to rest and then you're too keyed up, which leads to that 'tired but wired' feeling at night. If you're sleepy, like if you yawn and feel like you're going to go to sleep but find that you're just resting at night, it's important, but if you're not actually sleeping that's totally different for the body. So, if you're just resting but not actually sleeping then I want you to talk to a health care provider."

There Are Multiple Reasons for Sleep Issues, Including Hormonal Changes

Shelby explained to me that there are lots of other issues that can affect sleep, including whether or not you sleep with a bed partner, how your kids or other family members may be sleeping, and serious medical conditions. She explained,

> "Conditions like sleep apnea and restless leg syndrome get missed all the time. So, if you find that you're moving your legs or that like you just can't relax your body to go to sleep, bring that up to a doctor and consider going to a sleep clinic. If you think that you are waking with a dry mouth or you're having any pauses in your breathing that your spouse or bed partner notices, or if you're urinating a lot at night—those are all things to bring up and potentially have a sleep study to address. And sleep

studies can be done at home; they don't necessarily require going into a lab, depending on the severity."

I asked questions about the different sleep expertise that was out there. Admittedly, although I'd had some challenges with sleep during stressful periods of my life, I generally slept pretty well until I went through years of a sleep drought during my motherhood journey, including with my non-sleeping babies. I'd read or listened to almost everything about sleep hygiene. Including having a colder room, making sure screens are off at least an hour before bed, and avoiding alcohol at night. But Shelby, who is also a mother of three, broke it down in a very practical way that works for moms. She said,

> "Basic sleep hygiene doesn't fix insomnia, it fixes the people who don't make sleep a priority, but if you're someone who has insomnia, that stuff's not going to fix it. So, our society has gone from either not valuing sleep to almost an overcorrection or 'you have to sleep! Sleep so important, that if these things don't happen, you're going to die, or you're going to have dementia!' I think we need to be more realistic about it because society is not helping moms be able to make sleep a priority, and always, it's all of these white men who don't have kids, who are the ones that are preaching about it."

Sigh, yes, those are the experts I was listening to. I shared my list with her including what I had learned from reading a very popular sleep book.

She said,

> "It needs to be more realistic. Sleep's not going to be perfect every night so do what you can as often as you can to be a good sleeper. It may be five nights a week of being content with your sleep. So, take this into

account and rely on your community, your resources, or whatever you can to help. If you try all of that stuff and you're still struggling with your sleep or sleep quality, there are people like me, there are medical doctors and enough people who can help because there's always something that can be done. Whether it's napping, or getting rest, whatever it is, we just have to find that method to help you sleep a little bit better."

You Also Have Different Solutions, Depending on the Cause of Your Sleep Challenges

A good health care practitioner or doctor with expertise is a key part of navigating sleep troubles and will help you determine what makes the most sense based on your underlying needs and health. Shelby is a sleep psychologist who provides cognitive behavioral therapy for insomnia as a non-medicinal option that's highly effective for many people. But she explained, there are also approaches that involve medication and for those who are in perimenopause or menopause, hormone replacement therapy could potentially help address sleep issues. Again, why wing it? Talk to your primary care doctor or a health care practitioner for guidance on your specific needs.

Environment Change Can Bring Emotional Change

"Wow, you work there? How wonderful! I know how much you love food so it must be incredible to be there. I love their show, and I have so many of their cookbooks! What's it really like?" She asked. This was a conversation at a party with someone I didn't know very well. I wasn't sure if I wanted to give her the real answer, because I knew it would be somewhat disappointing, based on her reverence for the organization

I worked for at the time. But a long time ago, I made the commitment to myself to give others the "real answer" especially to direct questions, and to do so even when it was somewhat uncomfortable.

So, I said, "I really love the products and the quality of the work they do is excellent, which is what attracted me to apply there. I've also enjoyed getting to know many of the people and learning about their processes but it's not the right environment for me."

I enjoyed working with my direct team, and they were thrilled to have a manager concerned about their overall well-being and career growth, not just their work output, but the leadership team was a different story. When we had our weekly meetings, I felt like I was walking into a banking convention while wearing pink hair and roller skates. They had worked together for more than a decade. Despite the progress I made with my goals there, within a year, I knew it wasn't a fit and that was the first time I realized that I could love what a company does, without loving the company culture. After I left, once again I could admire their work from afar without the stifling feeling of being an employee.

We're a bit like plants. If we deprive ourselves for too long of sunlight, nutrients, water, or any of the ingredients we really need to flourish, we won't. I've talked a lot about the internal and systems reasons it's difficult to unlock ourselves from the imposed restrictions, even just what's considered "normal" in our society, even when it's not exactly healthy, reasonable, or right for us.

Learn What Environments Work for You and Why

Yes, where you work matters to your well-being, but also where you live. Not just the part of the world and city but your community and neighborhood. Maybe you would benefit from looking for a new, better, or less stressful job? Or remove something you no longer enjoy from your schedule. Remember, if your boat is too heavy and water is leaking in, don't try to bail out with a teacup! Treat stress like the emergency it really is until you are afloat again. At that point, reevaluate your commitments and decide if anything comes back onto your plate.

Overnights and Travel Can Offer Quick Resets

"Do I have to stay overnight? I'm still nursing and have never been away from the baby for more than an hour or two," I explained with some level of anguish in my voice. My boss explained that we had an off-site leadership meeting and that she'd like everyone to stay at the facility. Thankfully, it was not that far from where I lived, probably about 10 miles away on a college campus. But the 12 weeks of maternity leave after my son was born felt way too short. Although there were benefits to returning to work, and I appreciated eating lunch sitting down and going to the bathroom by myself, but having to leave my infant son overnight was a different story. I didn't feel ready for that.

Now, in hindsight, I realize I would never have "felt" ready. I fought against the idea of it whenever it was raised. Attending that off-site meeting was not what I wanted and at first, everything about it felt really foreign, including having so many adult conversations and sitting in the bright lights of the conference rooms. That first morning, however, when I woke up to complete silence having slept for almost five hours in a row, I felt better. After pumping milk, I was able to go for a run on my own early in the morning before meeting up with my colleagues for breakfast. The shift, being in a different place, having time primarily for myself and my job, felt pretty good. My husband and my mother took care of the baby and that forced separation from him allowed me to take care of myself in a better way, even though it was only for two days.

Business trips are unique because you're not paying the bill for the travel, and you are fully removed from the hands-on household and childcare responsibilities. Well, at least the physical part, even if it's rare to break free from the cognitive part. But unless you're attending a conference or internal meetings with breakfast through post-dinner activities, even though you're working, you will probably have more free time than you would at home. Much more.

I've also met mamas who have gone on girls' trips, romance revival trips with their partners, and even solo trips or group retreats shortly after their babies were born. In every case they've raved about having time away. So, let your needs guide you in the right direction and help you determine, based on your childcare setup, what's possible.

This has happened to me at points throughout my life—when I've started to feel stuck, lost, or tired, and suddenly the universe would deliver a situation where I had to leave my environment, usually to another city. But now I've been able to take this concept of the environment shift and activate it in small ways when I need a reset.

You Can Activate Micro-Changes to Your Environment at Any Time

Again, I'm not talking about a trip, or moving out of the country (although I fantasize about that more often these days), or even quitting your job. Your emotions will be up, down, and all over the place at times; it's the reality, especially for those of you who (like me) identify as type A achievement-oriented mamas. I'm sorry to say that even you will hit those weight-bearing emotional walls without warning. Here are a couple of quick, rescue remedies that I've found surprisingly effective.

So where do you go? In addition to all of the mental health support you can get your hands on—whether that's therapy, journaling, breathwork, prayer, or leaning into a faith community, you can make quick shifts to your environment at any time. I know, many of us want to make big changes when we're feeling stressed out, but as I shared in Section One, one of my go-to strategies is getting up and walking, especially if that's outside. Whether that's 5 minutes or 55 minutes, the fresh air and natural light will usually change your mood. You don't have to go full on forest bathing to experience the well-documented calming effects of nature.[2] If you're sitting, stand for a few moments, and if you're sitting or lying down, get up.

If you're exhausted and you have the ability to take a brief nap, go for it. There have been days when I'm either sleep deprived or ill, and I'll set a timer and lie down for 20 or 30 minutes, instead of trying to push through. If you have discretion over where you work, and are trying to reboot your productivity or clarity, consider working from a different room in your home or office. If you have coverage, and again, freedom to work from different spaces, then go to a library or coffee shop.

This can work if you're in a routine that doesn't serve you with the kids, too. Try taking them to a new environment, like a different play space, park, or room in your home, and you'll be surprised how well mini-resets can work. Catherine Hartley, an assistant professor in New York University's Department of Psychology, explained results from a research study she coauthored in a news release for New York University,[3] "Our results suggest that people feel happier when they have more variety in their daily routines—when they go to novel places and have a wider array of experiences."

Reclaim or Make Space Within Your Home

It's not just where you are, as you've probably guessed, but clearing your space and reducing clutter—aside from pleasing our inner battle cry for order—can also reduce anxiety. If you search for the "mental health benefits of decluttering" or even "tips on decluttering" you'll see this topic has been well covered. I won't dig into this in detail, but most of the research related to this[4] relies on the added mental bandwidth it takes from your brain to process and react to additional visual stimuli. Makes sense, right? You probably didn't need a research study to tell you how calming it feels to walk into a clear, clean space, ideally one that you didn't have anything to do with cleaning or clearing. But if you've been wondering how to shed the unease you feel with your workspace, play space, or favorite room, take the time to clear it out. A wonderful business coach I worked with a couple of years ago, Tara-Nicholle Kirke, CEO of SoulTour often said, "set a timer for 10 minutes and do a little bit of decluttering." I go through different areas of my space, very slowly when it feels important for my own sense of well-being, but it's rarely something I dedicate huge time blocks to anymore because it's less upsetting when the clearing doesn't stick. Better still if it's affordable, find a decluttering genius mom in your local area looking for freelance projects to do the work for you. Look for someone in your local parent groups, among your friends, or even search for her online. Trust me, with the popularity of outsourced home organizing, you will find her. About a year into the pandemic, I called in a local mom and decorator to address a long-standing stressor. Our place looked okay but wasn't functional in terms of storage or layout. Once my kids went from being toddlers to school-aged, although we no longer needed the pack-n-play or changing table, their toys sprawled across our condo more, and their clothes, shoes, athletic supplies, and book collections grew exponentially. They had a lot more stuff. It was gradual but when I realized our space no longer worked for our day-to-day reality, and it felt like it was an obstacle to getting through life's moments. I wanted someone who could reimagine it with more functionality despite the space limitations of condo living.

In addition to adding some bookshelves that run from ceiling to floor, I asked her for a room for myself to work. Okay, we didn't really have space for a real room, so I knew that wasn't possible, but I needed something. A closet, a corner... something that felt like mine. Something to ease the transition from being "away-at-the-office-unseen" mommy to "work-from-home-always-visible-and-interruptible" mommy. I needed structure to help make my new role, as a business owner, versus an employee who worked from home, to feel more permanent.

She gave me a little slice of our dining room and by little, I mean that I can't turn a cartwheel in this space but I'm now working behind a lovely fabric divider instead of at the end of the dining room table. I also have a real desk and a filing shelf with baskets organized into a few key categories. It's not the same as having a real home office with four walls and a door, but this set up, in conjunction with my occasional drop in to my local coworking space, has allowed me to feel more calm by not glancing constantly at the chaos of our home. Also, it helped to create a stable location for virtual meetings, my work-related paperwork, pens, journals, and other implements in one place that wasn't also serving as a meal, play, or sleeping space.

Manage Calendars and Expectations in Blended Families

There are a wide range of family structures[5] and blended families on the rise resulting in many aspects to our environments and family lives that we can't control, whether we gave birth, adopted, foster, became a parent through marriage, or some combination of these. But how much control you have, for example, over when you can go out of the country or how your holidays and evenings are structured, which in-laws you see or don't see, might be not be in your control if you're navigating shared custody arrangements with an ex or on behalf of your partner, who has an ex co-managing your schedule behind the scenes through a structured custody arrangement.

Friction is inevitable. But if your home life feels extra chaotic or unmanageable, then first pinpoint the sources of distress and talk with your partner, if you are partnered. Make sure that the two of you are aligned on schedules for at least the next three to six months, including your family priorities, and boundaries that are the most important for everyone involved. If you are not partnered, but you are subject to navigating your schedule with an ex or another adult who is part of your child's life, then similarly have an open conversation about your goals, needs, and see if you can align on what happens and when. If you don't feel well supported in that process, consider seeking out expert help such as a family therapist or mediator.

When your core schedule is more predictable, again knowing that nothing in mom-land is 100% predictable, find ways to carve your well-being space. That might be five minutes of deep breathing or calmly listening to music before enduring an emotional drop-off or pickup of your children. Or that might be taking a night to do something fun with a friend, call people who are closest to you, or take a class you've always wanted to take. Not every family environment is the same so, as always, choose your own adventure and look for every opportunity to find more ease and more peace, more often.

Notes

1. https://www.cdc.gov/sleep/data-research/facts-stats/adults-sleep-facts-and-stats.html
2. https://pubmed.ncbi.nlm.nih.gov/22948092/
3. https://www.nyu.edu/about/news-publications/news/2020/may/new-and-diverse-experiences-linked-to-enhanced-happiness--new-st.html
4. https://extension.usu.edu/mentalhealth/articles/the-mental-benefits-of-decluttering
5. https://www.pewresearch.org/social-trends/2023/09/14/the-modern-american-family/

Chapter 10

The Magic of Movement

"Yes, the funeral was so beautiful and so sad. There were so many people who spoke about her life and how much she meant to them. I wish you were here; I'm so happy that I went." My sister called me on her drive home. My aunt's niece, our cousin's cousin, passed away unexpectedly about two years ago. Although I hadn't seen her in decades, hearing about her sudden death struck me. She was close to my age and her kids are just a few years ahead of mine.

My sister went on to explain, "It was so inspiring to hear stories from her life. The church was full and so many people spoke about her impact, from her kids and husband to her coworkers, friends, and other family members."

What I heard was that everyone remembered how much she gave. She was an amazing daughter, mother, wife, sister, and friend. She was "organized" and "on top of everything" and "helpful" and "super involved" in her community, church, and full-time job.

She had a heart attack, and I can't help but think, what if she gave less to others and more to herself? What if everyone who was at that funeral had the opportunity, when she was alive to receive less and provide her with more help, would that have made a difference to her health? If so, would it have changed the beautiful legacy she's left behind?

Of course, there's no way to know this. What I do know, from speaking with her mother and my aunt, is that she was so busy taking care of so many people in her life that she wasn't spending time caring for her body. She wasn't feeling well yet delayed getting seen by a doctor until it was too late. Many of us—yes, including me—drift into treating our bodies like utility tools. Were you a Girl Scout? If so, do you remember the Swiss army knives we learned to use and carry? Make that lunch, finish that proposal, or pick up that prescription. Yet, any tool will break from overuse and lack of maintenance. Making it all work, such as motherhood, family life, community life, along with any kind of career, is *hard* to do—especially without the right support systems. And we continue to pay the penalty in our health. Being of service and being needed feels so glorious, it's almost like we're operating in our element. But choosing differently and prioritizing what really is critical and reasonable for your time, health, and resources to escape the "doing-it-all" toll is what this book, at its core, is all about. That's my deepest wish for you. In the next section, we'll start diving into how you can make a focus on your health a reality.

Plan a Walk (or Any Movement) Even If It's Within Your Home or Building

"What are you doing, Leslie?" One of my colleagues who had seen me down on the seventh floor, about 15 minutes later saw me back down there and, on my way, up to the eighth, where my office was. "Oh, I'm just getting in a little movement before my next meeting. I'm tired and getting in the steps helps." I explained cheerfully. He laughed and shook his head saying, "Cool. Maybe I'll join you next time!"

Remember I live in Boston, right? The weather here can be dreary during the winter and well, most of the year, except for the summer. In that particular job I was in meetings most of the day, many days of the week. Although I knew how to be strategic about blocking my calendar and grouping my meetings on certain days to protect deep work time, I wasn't in a psychologically safe situation at that point. My previous manager, who hired me was also a mom and a strong advocate, had left the company, and my new manager viewed "being in the office" as the holy grail for productivity. The culture was also completely "meeting centric" for my new area of responsibilities. I was leading a project with a lot of stakeholders and visibility. So, if I only had a 15-minute window, I used it to walk up and down the stairs between our floors in the building and that movement felt amazing. On days where I had more time, I would eat lunch at my computer and then take a walk outside for 20 or 30 minutes.

So, yes, walk up and down your stairs if you live inside of a single-family home with multiple levels or walk around your block or building. If you have a baby, put the baby in the stroller or baby sling to get yourself outside if you don't have or want childcare at that moment. I've also been known to do pushups in our narrow hallway while my child was on the potty or in the bathtub. I have done YouTube aerobic or high-intensity workout videos in the dining room while watching them on my phone or one of my children's iPads, even if it's for 5 or 10 minutes. I've also given myself the rule that every time I come out of the bathroom (when I'm at home) I need to do 10 jumping jacks.

Movement can be small and accessible and throughout the day versus one great big workout or exercise slot. It's true,

I love my run every morning because it's medicine to me, but I also do lots of small movements throughout the day. Now that I have a tracker on my watch, I know I cover a lot of steps during the average day even if I don't intend to just based on these little rules and rituals I've made for myself.

Tackle Errands on Foot When Possible

"Mom, what do you mean it's *down the street*?" my daughter asked and eyed me with suspicion. She turned to my son and said, "Mom says, 'down the street'. . . what do you think that means?" My son started laughing and said, "well, it must be in a neighboring state then, perhaps New York?" My kids have a running joke that I say everything is down the street because whether it's a 5-minute or a 25-minute walk I still consider it reasonable to walk there. I remember when each of them were toddlers I was so proud that I didn't need to bring a stroller with me. They could walk all the way to one of the further grocery stores about a mile away. Since I am pretty blessed with good health I can walk just about everywhere, and I do. We don't have a car anymore full-time, and when we did, we barely drove it. Last year, we leased a car during the heavy driving months of travel soccer season. I realize, however, this doesn't work for everybody. I can walk to a local playground within about two minutes, or to a really good restaurant or my favorite bookstore within 15 minutes. With most of the choices (i.e., which grocery story, class, or post office) I will prioritize proximity over "excellence" in some cases because of the convenience. For example, I know there may be a better karate school, but if it's 5 or 10 miles away versus a half a mile away, the closer one is the better fit. Now, if either of my kids were child prodigies in karate, I would reevaluate our options, but making this decision makes life's logistics easier—especially now that they are in so many activities.

Choose Easy Exercise over Your Favorite Exercise

"What am I going to do now? I'm 32!" I practically shrieked my deepest fear, growing older without the kids I always wanted. My therapist said, "Leslie, I don't think you're depressed in a clinical sense, but it's understandable that you're feeling down. What about your anxiety; have you always been anxious?" she asked.

I carefully pulled the sheet of yellow notebook paper from inside of my planner. I had written a categorized list of things I wanted to address with my new therapist. At that point, my only experience with therapy was going through couples therapy with my soon-to-be ex-husband. He had moved out about a month before I started seeing her and I was emotionally drained by the idea of having failed at marriage. I sighed and said, "Honestly, I would have never described myself that way but as I look at some of the problems I'm dealing with right now and where I'd like to see changes a lot of it probably is about managing anxiety. I feel driven to do things to a high standard, and I'm certainly 'type A' but perhaps that 'A' is really for anxiety."

She responded, "I'd like you to consider medication, Leslie. It's an option that works for a lot of people, but I'll be candid it typically takes six to eight weeks and there's some trial and error." I interrupted her, "No, I don't think so." I thought about the many members of my family that I had watched struggle with getting the right medications for their mental health. I didn't want to go through that, on top of what I was already going through. I explained, "Listen, I don't even like to take aspirin. I don't like the idea of taking anything that is manufactured or unnatural, so I'd rather only consider that as a last resort."

She looked me in the eye and said, "Well, I understand that and based on where you are right now, it's only a suggestion, but it may be necessary for us to revisit to help you get into a better place. However, an alternative is regular exercise. There are studies that have shown exercising three or more days a week is as effective as medication for some people with mild to moderate anxiety or depression."

Wait, what? Exercise... I love exercise! That winter I did spend a lot of time ice skating and I was a competitive dancer and active for most of my life until I entered corporate life after college. Suddenly, trying to prove myself professionally meant being chained to a desk most days and only taking the occasional step class or dance outing with friends. I wasn't motivated to experiment with anything but increasing my time on work back then. "Okay, I'll do that." I had recently moved back to Boston after a nearly three-year expat assignment in London. I originally moved there for work with my now ex, but it was clear that we were holding onto a relationship that was in critical condition so, shortly after we moved back to the United States we split. Although at this point, I was getting a lot of physical activity working in the pastry kitchen at the Ritz after a rather radical career change from corporate life to food, but I hadn't found a new gym.

The next day, I enrolled at a local gym for women. I didn't want to be in a space with men, because at that point, I was uninterested in having anyone try to chat me up. I just wanted to drag myself through a workout with sloppy gym clothes, no makeup, and no qualms about it. Although my therapist recommended three times per week, in my typical type A fashion, I started working out every day. That was the beginning of my running practice. Despite abandoning the track team in seventh grade because they made us train outside in the frigid New York winters, I've always liked running. After working out on the fancy machines at the gorgeous women's gym, and sampling almost every kickboxing, aerobics, and core class they had, I knew that ultimately to stay with my daily practice it had to be easy. And by easy, I mean, no equipment, court times, tee times, commutes, or other complicated logistics that will rule it out more often than not.

This is the main point: if you don't already have a regular movement practice, let's get you fully into "the thing" that's your physical activity with greater ease and joy. Do you want better energy? How about control over self-destructive tendencies, like having to-do lists the length of the Dead Sea scrolls? Eager to dial down that "what-if" energy from going to full-worry mode? Remember, health for moms is this ministry, and movement is medicine. It's the number one most effective thing I do to manage mental and physical health, and it can be for you, too.

Establish a Daily Movement Practice

I slipped out the door quietly and started putting on my sneakers. It was still dark in our hallway, but it was light enough for me to run outside instead of going over to the gym. I could hear crying, and I froze. No, no, no! She should not be awake right now! I held my breath and waited, hoping that it would stop or that my husband would wake up and soothe our daughter back to sleep. The crying continued escalating. I looked at my watch. I really only had about 35 minutes left before I had to leave for an early meeting downtown. Shit. I muttered under my breath. I went back inside and swooped up my baby girl. Her face was full of smiles and she held onto me like a lifeline. I told her that we were going to go running today. She started whispering, "Jor . . . Jor . . . George!" George; oh dear, I went back. How could I forget about Curious George? I grabbed him, along with a sweater and her winter hat. I brought her into the kitchen, holding her in one arm while I hastily threw a bunch of small crackers into a snack pack with the other. Between the winter sleep bag on the stroller, her hat, snack pack, and small water bottle she was good to go, but it cost about 10 minutes of time so, I pushed to get out the door a little faster so we could get at least a mile or two in. I brought down the rain shield because it started misting ever so slightly, some sort of gray snow/rain slurry. I stopped by a tree paused so she could see the rabbits coming out from under their burrows and zipping through the neighborhood. Even though running with my daughter was not my plan and nor was it nearly as head cleansing as running alone, we got it done and there was always something magical about seeing her eyes light up, watching nature right there with me in the quietest time of day.

I run every day and it's my anchor. This has been consistent through heavy travel periods, inconsistent childcare or none at all, family emergencies, and family vacations. When I was pregnant or nursing an injury, I replaced running with walking. You can create your own movement practice that works well for you.

Have you ever read *Atomic Habits* by James Clear? I loved the book but a lot of his advice as written doesn't work for most mothers, in part because it relies on tapping our sources of internal motivation or willpower with external structure. It's not like that's a bad thing, but again, for most moms willpower isn't the real problem: discretionary time is. Which means we need to do things differently, like line up childcare and other supports, or trim activities down in size and plan ahead for schedule conflicts. I particularly liked his section about what works to cement a new habit or behavior. In the book, he explains that daily habits can be easier to establish than periodic ones, and cites the research behind it. Interestingly, when we launched the Mom's Hierarchy of Needs web app TimeCheck®, I started it thinking it would be great to give moms an easy way to check in on their top of the hierarchy activities once per week and get a personal read out with ideas on how to make more time for self-care.

In the testing phase, I got a ton of feedback from the 50 moms in our advisory group and several other friends, colleagues and, of course, my sister. Several moms asked for a daily check-in instead so they could set the habit more easily and not spend too much time calculating what they did over the course of a week. I didn't expect people to want that, but once I learned why, the lightbulb went off: I considered how my own running habit stuck so well precisely because it's daily. So, I asked the engineers to also build a daily option. Daily may seem like a lot, if you're not doing any movement or exercise now, but think about how many other routines you've woven into your life each day? You can always experiment with it for a month and then decide if it suits your needs long term.

How to Set Yourself Up for Daily Movement Success

- **Start your day with movement** (or as soon as possible after you wake up). Allocate this time for yourself, however, when your life is mom-dynamic, be prepared that it will change more often than you might like. Later I'll provide steps on how to do this and set yourself up for the anticipated changes in advance. In my world right now, my run is usually after dropping off the kids during the school week (plan A), or on the weekends, it's often before they wake up, if they're sleeping later (plan B), but my daughter tends to wake up early a lot, so it's typically after I've made breakfast (plan C). If I'm on a business trip, then it really is an entire morning routine of "me things" and running comes after a brief visualization or meditation and journaling, but very early in the morning (plan D). When my kids were toddlers and babies, often as I shared they had to come with me in the running stroller and later, I'd run behind them on their bikes or scooters (plan E). Sometimes, it's for a glorious 45 minutes and other times, it's for 10 minutes. Your time and approach will have to be conditional based on what is happening with your family, health, or your work schedule. That's okay; just plan for that each time.

- **Make it close by.** Your core exercise of choice needs to be within a 10- to 15-minute *walk* of where you live. Okay, let me explain. That doesn't mean you necessarily need to find a gym that's within 15 minutes; it means that if you live in the middle of nowhere and need a car to go anywhere, your exercise of choice might need to be walking outside, a YouTube HIIT routine in your kitchen, using a treadmill or bike in your home, lifting weights (or laundry detergent bottles; yep, I've done it) or running up and down stairs in your apartment building. It must be something you can turn on quickly and not need to rely on a commute to get there.
- **Make it (almost) equipment free.** Basically, you want whatever you choose to be portable for when you're out of town or just away from your normal environment. This doesn't mean you can't enjoy your mountain bike, meet up with your bestie for pickleball, take a dance class, or join that fancy gym you've been eyeing with the cucumber water. It only means that your main thing that you do has to be something easier than any of that to implement. When you insert anything more complicated than a pair of sneakers or a portable small piece of equipment (think a jump rope or rubber resistance band) your workout becomes very fixed and fragile if it has to happen in a certain place or under certain atmospheric conditions.
- **Create energetic space for it.** When you pick your plan A schedule, choose a time when you have childcare (and/or eldercare, if that applies) and the appropriate amount of energy and time to get in the flow of the activity, or at the very least complete it in the way that feels optimal to you. I explain the concept of "energetic space" in much more detail at the end of this chapter so you can put these ideas together, and in the Afterword, I provide you with a link to the systems guide for it. For now, bear in mind you need more than one plan with kids.

- **Check your calendar the night before.** It seems obvious but make a quick check of your calendar a part of your pre-bedtime routine. It's amazing how often something unplanned (e.g., that dentist visit you scheduled six months ago) or sudden (mandatory department meeting called for 9 a.m.) can change what you expect your day to look like. Plan your wake-up time accordingly.
- **Also have a plan B and plan C time.** I know, you had everything scheduled just so and then one little shift unraveled the entire thing! No worries because you have your plan B time, remember? It removes some of that anxiety we feel when things go wrong, because, of course, it's unavoidable that not everything will follow the plan.
- **Prepare for weather variations if your exercise is outside.** Yes, you also need a plan A, B, or C outfit that suits the environment depending on what your movement is. Unless you live someplace with consistently beautiful weather (unlike Boston) you will need a foul weather backup. Then, the inevitable snow/sleet/rain/wind/ice storm that comes up will not threaten your movement time.

After the pandemic, I became an all-weather runner. Before that, I would go to the gym (a short walk) when the weather was bad. So, I invested in waterproof sneakers, ice grips for my sneakers—Yaktrax is the brand I buy, recommended by the fabulous Dr. April Seifert whom I mentioned in Section One. They're snow-amazing.

I also bought a windbreaker that is waterproof, a water-resistant light down jacket, long underwear for when it's under 20 degrees, a waterproof hat for rain running, and glove liners. So, basically, I have a set of variables and know exactly how I'm going to have to dress. See the following list for a guide. Now this may not work for you, based on where you live and how cold or wet it gets, but you can adapt this for your situation.

Outdoor running/ walking	Under 30 degrees F	30–45 degrees F	45–60 degrees F	60+ degrees F
Dry	– Fleece leggings or leggings with long underwear – Base layer T-shirt, turtleneck, long underwear/thermal hoodie, lined waterproof windbreaker jacket – Glove liners and thick gloves (both are in my pockets; I use the glove liners only if it's below 15 degrees F) – Knit, lined winter hat (Grace Eleyae)	– Thick long leggings – Base layer T-shirt, turtleneck, lined waterproof windbreaker – Glove liners – Knit, lined winter hat (Grace Eleyae)	– Midweight long leggings – T-shirt or long sleeved T-shirt with sweatshirt or lined jacket – Hairband (hair wrapped underneath)	– Cropped lighter weight or midweight leggings – T-shirt – Headband
Wet	– Fleece leggings or leggings with long underwear – Base layer T-shirt, turtleneck, lined waterproof windbreaker, or light down water-resistant jacket – Glove liners – Waterproof sneakers – Waterproof hat (Hairbrella)	– Thick long leggings – Base layer T-shirt, turtleneck, lined waterproof windbreaker – Glove liners – Hairband (hair wrapped underneath)	– Midweight long leggings – T-shirt or long sleeved T-shirt with sweatshirt or lined jacket – Waterproof hat (Hairbrella)	– Cropped lighter weight or mid-weight leggings – T-shirt – Waterproof hat (Hairbrella)

Outdoor running/ walking	Under 30 degrees F	30–45 degrees F	45–60 degrees F	60+ degrees F
Snowy/Icy	- Fleece leggings or leggings with long underwear - Base layer T-shirt, turtleneck, lined waterproof windbreaker or light down water-resistant jacket - Glove liners - Knit, lined winter hat (Grace Eleyae) - Regular or waterproof sneakers with ice grips (I use Yaktrax)	Thick long leggings - Base layer T-shirt, turtleneck, lined waterproof windbreaker - Glove liners Hairband (hair wrapped underneath)		

- **Wear (some of) your workout clothes to bed.** I feel you wincing—so *unsexy Leslie*—but believe me, if you have to fiddle around to find a sports bra and workout clothes in the dark wee hours of the morning without waking your partner (if you have one) or children, you will realize how brilliant this move is! Not to mention, strong is the new sexy! I also put everything I don't wear to bed (fleece, headband, socks, etc.) next to or under the bed in an easy-to-reach spot.
- **Plans D and/or E.** Have a with-kids plan. For me that was having a running stroller once my kids were old enough. Before that it was running on the treadmill at home with the baby in the bouncy chair. If your child or youngest child is a baby or toddler, a running stroller is a must (after they're about nine months old). I loved my BOB stroller and it was a big part of my weekend running routine.

Call it exercise, working out, or just a commitment to move your body more often and with more intention. You will begin to feel the benefits in ways that permeate your daily experience. You may be wondering, "but, Leslie, where am I going to get all this energy to increase movement or start working out every day?" Well, I'm happy you asked because there's another important source of fuel we haven't discussed yet. You probably knew that somewhere in this book I was going to talk about your options for food and nutrition. Now, don't get worried that it's going to be preachy; it's not. I promise there are flexible ways for you to think about and incorporate different inputs, including food, which is the focus of our next chapter in ways that can increase your energy, save time, and ultimately, decrease complexity.

Chapter 11

Manage Energy Inputs Including Your Nutrition and Hormonal Health

Streamline and Systematize Meals

"Les, I need your recipe. Can you send it to me?" My cousin sent me a nice text after I gifted her homemade granola when my son and I returned from the visit to her house over the summer. I responded, "I can send you the recipe Al, just give me a little bit of time." I was trying to create some buffer—not that it was a lot of work, but I didn't want to sit down and document the whole recipe unless I really had the time to do so, but she pressed with another text and said, "I really want to make it this weekend."

As you may recall from Chapter 3, this is my same cousin who jokingly called me the "Pioneer Woman" because I didn't want to use her boxed pancake mix. Well, now she is a very happy batch granola maker, and she does not enjoy cooking.

So, if you enjoy granola as much as I do, you'll know there are lots of different little variations in how it can be done. So, choose your own adventure if you decide to make it, because store-bought granola is not worth your time or money when you find out how easy it is to make. Plus you will be so much happier with the quality. Pro tip: I add a couple of teaspoons of crushed cardamom to mine along with walnuts, pepitas, almonds, and a generous topping of chia seeds after it's been baked. The kids get oatmeal most days, but on the weekends they have their "treat days" as far as their breakfast is concerned. It started years ago, perhaps not surprisingly as my husband's idea, to have pancakes on Saturdays, which turned into Saturdays and Sundays. Then, after I perfected my version of a (slightly) healthier pancake variation (I subbed out about 40% of the all-purpose flour for almond flour) that's still light, fluffy, and delicious, the kids somehow decided they wanted Belgian waffles instead. So, I went through this whole waffle testing phase on the weekends for months and now, perhaps because I perfected that, they've moved on to homemade brioche French toast. No, I'm not making this up, I really do make the brioche for the French toast . . . but I've systematized that, too. I make three loaves at a time and freeze them, after the first rise so, basically, I'm only making a big batch of brioche every three weeks and the anglaise for the French toast is quite easy to make each week. It takes less time than making pancakes and I also do a double batch so it lasts Saturday and Sunday. Okay, back to the granola, that's what I eat for breakfast on the weekends or when I'm in a hurry. Like the days I have early conferences or when I'm running late to a soccer or basketball game and need to take something for breakfast to eat from the sidelines. It's delightful with Greek yogurt and fresh fruit, and it's so easy because I make a huge batch of that every two to three weeks. The point of this story is not to freak you out about feeling the need to make homemade everything; remember you don't have to. But there are staples that are surprisingly easy to make, and if you decide to do so, you can batch cook, batch bake, batch freeze, or batch prep them. Even though there are some pricey ingredients, like nuts in the granola, compared to a high-quality artisan or bakery version, it's much less expensive, fresher, doesn't have any preservatives in it, and I've added a lot of good-for-you ingredients like the variety of nuts and avocado oil (versus seed oils) not to mention the chia seeds I sprinkle on top at the end.

I am on the extreme end of the cooking spectrum. As I shared pre-kids, food was my hobby, and I have a culinary degree. I almost started a food company with my friend Lori several years ago and I pull recipes and menus together for the fun of it. I know it's not desirable for most moms to do that much cooking from scratch, but you don't have to be a "pioneer woman" to have food work in favor of your health or develop systems that make it easier to have healthy meals, without the same stress of needing to deal with the "what's for dinner" question at the last possible minute—whether you make them or simply assemble them.

I grew up eating delicious home-cooked meals most of the time. Despite being transplanted to one of the coldest corners of the United States, just outside of Rochester, New York, my mother tried valiantly to grow fruit trees in our Fairport, New York, yard. We had an apple tree, a pear tree, peaches, and plums, and one year, she even made a bold attempt to grow mangoes that didn't quite work out. She made our ice cream, often using the ingredients that grew in our yard, including crabapple ice cream, which may sound gross but trust me, she made it delicious. Mum added seasoning and spices to everything, including her version of American classics like burgers or potato salad. As a child, I didn't love all of the Bajan foods, like flying fish or pigs feet, but I came to appreciate most of them, especially flying fish, and learned to make some of my favorite Caribbean meals as an adult.

Food and the nutrition we derive from it also has a profound impact on our health. Having good-quality food tends to be less costly and complicated overall because control over your time often means controlling easy variables like not having to go to pick up takeout, return to the grocery store a third time, or my favorite, making dinner at 10 p.m. On a school night. It doesn't have to be fancy to be effective. There are many nights I've made omelets and a salad for dinner because it takes less than 15 minutes. In the most recent wave of our now post-pandemic research study, most moms (52%) want to "eat differently" as part of their self-care routine. Although food, in the form of healthier meals, is often a top item on the self-care wish list across our studies, like fitting in exercise or doctors' appointments, the issue for most of us is time.

Treat Food Like the Powerful Energy Source It Is

Meal management for a family is intense. From the cooking, grocery buying, food prep, clean up, and inventory management, it's like taking on a never-ending, part-time job. Which is why so many parents have a love–hate relationship with meals. I assure you, you don't need to be interested in making everything from scratch or even doing real cooking to have healthier options that work within your schedule, needs, and budget.

Everything we put into our bodies affects our well-being. Nutrient-rich, high-quality food is a leveraged use of your time to protect your energy and well-being over the short and longer terms. What's tricky it that "eating well" can really vary by person. There is no "ideal diet" that works universally for everyone. There are diets widely accepted as being beneficial to cardiovascular, mental, and physical health of most people. For example, you may have heard about the Mediterranean diet because it's often recommended as a way to eat that is considered (and proven) to be healthiest for most people. I like this description of it from the American Heart Association[1]: "A Mediterranean-style diet typically includes: plenty of fruits, vegetables, bread and other grains, potatoes, beans, nuts and seeds; olive oil as a primary fat source; and dairy products, eggs, fish and poultry in low to moderate amounts. Fish and poultry are more common than red meat in this diet. It also centers on minimally processed, plant-based foods. Wine may be consumed in low to moderate amounts, usually with meals. Fruit is a common dessert instead of sweets."

If you have an underlying medical condition, for example, you're allergic to fish, then it doesn't matter what the experts say, fish clearly won't make you healthier! Diabetics need to avoid sugar and carbohydrate-laden food in a way that non-diabetics generally do not. With that said, let me put a few caveats in place. Food matters a lot; that's my main point here. But I'm a food enthusiast not a nutritionist. In culinary school we learned how to make tasty things quickly and efficiently. There are so many good books about nutrition and even specific diets that I will not spend much time covering this territory in this book.

What I will share is philosophies, key information, and systems to make the time to eat well. You need to know why healthier food matters to your health and health span and evolve a system you can use to save time by making healthier meals. This involves cooking if you want it to, but if you're savvy about using prepared foods, which are now widely available, from meal kits or grocery stores, you can also assemble your meals. You can still buy convenience foods or order takeout when the mood strikes you. I do that from time to time, too. But it can be your choice; you don't have to feel trapped in a cycle of food decisions that are either expensive for your budget or not good for your health and wellness because of what they put in it to make it tasty or preserve it. You know what I'm talking about: the extra stuff that some fast, convenient, packaged, processed, or restaurant meals contain, that isn't really the type of thing you want to ingest on a regular basis. Read the labels when you're at the store from time to time. You will see hard-to-pronounce words that do not sound at all appetizing. Use that as a flag right there.

How can you begin to eat differently? Here are the principles you can consider to make meals healthier and realistic, with the type of schedules we keep. A detailed systems guide along with a few family-friendly recipes is also linked for you in the Afterword.

Plan Meals with Microbiome Health in Mind

You may hear about "gut health," as it's a topic of discussion in nutritional and mental health circles more and more often. There are excellent reasons for this, and I'll share a few key points I've learned during interviews with experts in this area, in addition to reading through a dizzying amount of secondary research studies. Here's a brief excerpt from my discussion with Heather Wise and information from her book, *A Gut Feeling: Conquer Your Sweet Tooth by Tuning into the Microbiome*.[2] Heather said, "It's a commitment, but an intentional focus on making our gut biome stronger can make us more invincible to modern changes in our world." Encouraging news! She wrote, "Our bodies are incredibly resilient. We have detox pathways built in to eliminate the harmful chemicals that enter our systems. We just need to support it by letting it do its job by consuming different types of unpasteurized and fermented foods that encourage healthy bacteria to thrive."

I've been doing this intentionally since I first interviewed Heather in 2019. She described how accessible this is. There are very simple recipes for fermented foods, high in the "good bacteria" our microbiomes need to remain strong and fight off toxins, like sauerkraut. During our conversation, she also explained how to create a "kavass," which something I wasn't familiar with, by using beets[3] or other vegetables "high in natural sugar that feed on the probiotics in the air."

Prepared fermented foods are also widely available, so if the idea of making your own doesn't appeal, check your local grocer for kimchi or sauerkraut (two examples I like personally) that are made with high-quality ingredients. In the interview, Heather went on to explain, "Supplements might have one strain of good bacteria, versus homemade kavass, which might have dozens or even hundreds of different strains." She said a good prebiotic green drink might have thousands. In general, "fresh drinks like green smoothies or a green prebiotic drink made from whole foods are more effective than a probiotic supplement." Heather shared, "In my experience and those of my clients, green prebiotic powders can be just as effective, if not more so, than fermented foods." She mentioned her daughter loves the Green Vibrance Kids' mix and said, "The kid's version is suitable for the whole family and you can drink a prebiotic green drink every day."

I also began using Green Vibrance (easy to find online or at certain grocery stores) as part of my daily routine, after meeting with her because I'd rather cover the nutritional bases from a prebiotic and probiotic standpoint with something easy to prepare. I haven't been able to convince my kids to drink it yet (it's a very green-looking drink) but I've put prebiotics and probiotics into the family diet in other ways and the kids take kid-friendly supplements.

Avoid Toxicity in Foods (and Other Products)

Okay, although it's not the focus of this book, I do spend more time than I care to admit researching what types of foods, food packaging, and products are more likely to contain toxins, artificial dyes, or chemicals because there's a disturbing amount of bad things inside of foods we buy. Personally, I believe there's not enough attention focused on this. You want to make choices about your body and what goes into it with clarity. I care much more about these things than I do about the presence of natural sugar or fat for that matter. Let's just say, I'd much rather have a plate of bacon than cereal with red dye number 3. You may not want to geek out on this sort of thing and if so, I get it . . . we have plenty to worry about already. But if you're interested in having a resource, there's a good recap of food toxins that are both known (like BPA and mercury) and less known, in this Healthline Article,[4] which makes them easier to avoid. Also, I'm a big fan of the Environmental Working Group's[5] website, where they review common household products, including food, skin and beauty products, in addition to having a guide about local tap water. It's easy to use when you're researching a new or existing product and can either create comfort or prompt a switch to something better.

Give Your Food Favorites a Healthier Upgrade

"Oh my goodness this is so delicious . . . really, it doesn't have any dairy in it? Leslie, can I have the recipe?" I was about to respond but another one of my son's classmates came by with his plate and asked me, "Can I please have another piece?" I sliced him another smaller piece of chocolate cake and he left with a big smile on his face. We had a little parent and family gathering for my son's kindergarten class and it was delightful to see people for more than a few minutes during drop-off or pickup and to get all the kids together. It was wild, boisterous, but really fun. My daughter was also learning how to walk then, so I remember spending a good amount of time at the party just holding her hands while we walked up and down the stairs together. We live in a condo, as I mentioned, and do not have stairs inside of our unit so, the whole idea of a staircase was mythical to her. I was tired of walking her up and down the stairs but certainly recognized that the steps were not so bad for me to fit in either.

No one really understood how I took that chocolate cake and made it so rich and inviting despite the fact that it didn't have any dairy in it. When my daughter was two weeks old, I had to rush her to the hospital with a distended belly. Thankfully, after 4 days of tests we learned it was a milk allergy but it lasted for a year and a half so while I was nursing, I could not have anything dairy related either. I had to learn to take just about all of my favorite foods and turn them into dairy-free versions, including that chocolate cake. Coconut milk replaced the heavy cream to make the chocolate ganache frosting and coconut oil was used instead of butter. The whole thing turned out beautifully (chocolate is my go-to for an impressive dessert). Before my daughter was born, when we had friends visit with their daughter who couldn't enjoy dairy, I made her a special chocolate ice cream that used a coconut cream base, and she was very happy with it. Did it taste exactly like traditional chocolate ice cream? No. However, it was still really good and creamy.

Food is deeply personal, but also cultural and social. Many of us have our early memories from family gatherings, eating foods we love then, and often we still find those foods comforting when we plan meals for ourselves and our families. If you are also from an immigrant background, many of us have really flavorful and interesting foods from our cultures that we want to keep eating, even if they're not exactly health foods. I had the pleasure of speaking with Sue-Ellen Anderson-Haynes, MS, RDN, CDCES, a Registered Dietary Nutritionist, diabetes and women's health expert, and the CEO of 360° Girls & Women, LLC a holistic health and wellness company, about how to think about your options when it comes to diets and nutrition. After spending years working in hospital systems and her continued work to help people, including those with chronic medical conditions, adapt or change their diets she learned how to tune in to this need and do so in a way that was accessible. She said, "I talk with my patients all the time about cooking techniques and portion control." Sue-Ellen is from Jamaica originally and my family is Bajan, so during our interview we discussed a lot of Caribbean foods, including black cake, which is very popular in the region. It's rich, delicious but high in sugar and very popular during the holidays. She suggested, for high-calorie or high-fat foods, that we consider having less than we usually would. Or, selecting a special event—like a holiday, anniversary, or birthday—where you indulge in that food once or twice per year. Other dishes that are meaningful to your family or culture can be adapted by how you cook them. As she and I discussed, you can use a different type of cooking oil with less saturated fats or use an air fryer versus frying in oil at all. She added, "You can also keep your herbs and spices so, if you're making a curry and you're trying to cut down on the amount of food, calories, or fat that you're using, maybe you want to go with a plant base. If you're saying, 'oh, I still enjoy curry; it's a particular spice from my culture', we're not telling you to get rid of curry. You can still have the spices, but the question is, what are you using the curry with?" Indeed, you can alternate having curried goat and curried cauliflower or eggplant.

Sue-Ellen explains, "So, I'm a plant-based dietitian and there isn't one diet that can fit everybody, as you know, but we know that research says the more plants you're eating, that's best for your gut, your brain, and your heart. Now I'm not going to advise you to become a vegan, but you should aim to have a majority, I usually recommend 70–80% of your food intake come from plants. This includes beans, nuts, fruits, whole grains, and vegetables."

We also discussed ketogenic diets, because they've become wildly popular, and there are many people who advocate for them. Sue-Ellen, however, does not recommend them, unless it's medically necessary. And with any major dietary changes, it should be done under medical supervision. She explained,

> "The keto diet is a very low carb diet, and you're burning fat as fuel. The only time I recommend a keto diet is if you have a medical condition, like epilepsy, and it's medically necessary. Some research is saying that keto diets, specifically mainly those with plant-based fats, may be helpful to your brain health because fats that are rich in omega threes are good for your brain and it's good to increase those. That doesn't mean, however, you cut out all of the other foods with carbohydrates and just eat those because you're going to miss that important fuel for the brain and red blood cells."

She went on to explain that going into ketosis can be very dangerous, especially for people with type 1 diabetes, where it can be fatal; so again, before trying a new way of eating or making big changes, talk to your doctor or health care practitioner to make sure it's a good fit for your health and needs.

Spice-It-Up Food for the Adults with Simple Tweaks

Okay, kid-friendly food can get very dull, very fast. I mean, how many times can you have chicken or turkey especially forgoing your favorite spices like garlic, turmeric, or cumin? Salt and pepper are lovely but used sparingly and with simple preparations (e.g., sauceless for my kiddos) you can lose some of that fun, flavorful food magic that makes mealtime so delightful. In the systems guide I provide the link for in the Afterword is an expanded version of the "how to save time making family dinner guide" that is based on one of the first articles I wrote for

Mom's Hierarchy of Needs. You'll see some recommendations you can put into practice. There are modifications for just about everything you can imagine to add the spice at the end and remove the kids' portions, if necessary, at the right time so you can put all of the chili peppers, curry, garlic, sage, onions, or other fabulous meal-making-flavors in there for yourself and your partner, if you have one.

By the Way, You Don't Need to Be the Food Person If You Are Partnered

If you have a partner who is healthy and capable of assisting with meals, you don't have to be the one to make, plan, organize, and otherwise curate food. Yes, it's still a gendered task in most families but that's just a legacy of the way we were conditioned. Food can be anyone's role. Subsets of the responsibilities can also be assigned to someone else; for example, you might be very happy to grocery shop from a list and make sure food is in the home yet have no involvement in preparing it. You can also be the person to cook only, and not do any of the cleanup, overall meal planning, inventory management, or grocery shopping. Remember the household manager role option from Section Two? Well, that's one way to outsource some portion of this. I've also met people who have found great local meal services, private chefs, or restaurants that provide accessibly priced, well-balanced family meals. So if you can outsource this in a reasonable way, go for it! My sister, who does not like to cook by the way, started training my nieces to cook by sending them to kids cooking classes during the summers when they were in middle school. So, now that they are in their late teens, they can cook, bake, and often make desserts and treats. I personally love food and love to cook and my husband also loves food and loves to cook. He's an excellent cook actually but the type of cooking he does isn't as (ahem . . . the word I'm looking for here is healthy) or practical for the daily rhythm of a family. So, between the two of us, I'm the healthier cook because I am very excited to read a lot of the nutritional guidelines, the underlying research, and have made that type of digging into everything associated with food a lifelong pursuit. I'm in the better position to have this responsibility in our family but in your family, your partner may be the one to tap for this, or if you have older kids, who are ready to upskill, then they can become part of the meal-making responsibilities and extended team.

Make One Meal for Everyone (with Tweaks)

Tap into one dinner energy. Seriously. Do you make individual dinners that cater to each and every eater in the family? Right. It's a thing, I've seen it done but I'm saying, no more of that; you are not a short order cook! My kids ask me to do this sometimes and I remind them, they do not live adjacent to a diner. Some of this requires just telling your family no and holding tight onto the boundary that you are not going to personalize their meals like they're ordering from a restaurant; you will not spend your precious time and energy that way, and when you say it you have to mean it. Being able to do this, however, means being able to create the kid-friendly version of meals that are suitable for adults. Think about this example: make your braised chicken thighs, in apple cider or fresh orange juice and cumin, and then remove all of them from the pan. Put enough chicken aside for your kids, so you can cut them into smaller pieces if necessary. In the meanwhile, you take the remaining cooking liquid that's in the pan and add spicy grainy French mustard, a chopped garlic clove, and a little dash of your favorite heat (mine is Bajan pepper sauce) such as Sriracha, dried red chili pepper flakes, or something else entirely.

Hormonal Health—Another Important Fuel Source for Female Bodies

"Leslie, how old are you, if you don't mind me asking?" A colleague asked me this question on a group conference call so, yes, I did mind her asking. I was mortified. Not because I was embarrassed about my age, but I was a consultant working with a client team of mostly men, who were all on the call with us. The reality is, I already felt vulnerable about being different. But I answered her anyway; at the time, I was 47.

This came up because I made a casual comment during the chitchat before the call officially started about waking up at about 2 a.m. and being unable to get back to sleep. I explained, it was becoming a regular occurrence that I wasn't at all happy with, especially now that my kids were actually sleeping through the night after years of sleep struggle. The colleague was an obstetrician–gynecologist (OB-GYN) and our medical consultant on the team. She explained, "Leslie, you're probably going through perimenopause; it's totally normal. There's a natural drop in estrogen that affects sleep."

Wait, what? Receiving a surprising personal diagnosis on a group conference call felt super awkward. But learning this little health fact, quite by accident, was a gift that I later appreciated. I called my sister about it the next day and felt like I should call every woman I knew in her forties at the time because suddenly I had some new information that I could research to help untangle the mysterious sleep issue.

Estrogen[6] is a bit like oxygen for female bodies. And when it naturally declines, along with its companion progesterone,[7] it affects every system in our bodies. So, hot flashes[8] are only a small part of the larger story about treatment. Although it can happen earlier or later, perimenopause, aka pre-menopause, tends to start in our forties. And can last for 10 years before menopause. During that time, insomnia and sleep disruption[9] is common. But even if your sleep is solid, the hormonal shifts alone can increase mood swings, anxiety, depression,[10] or rage. So, be proactive with your doctors and health care providers about your mental and physical health needs. Especially if you've had a history of depression.[11]

An interview with Dr. Sophia Yen, founder of Pandia Health, physician, professor, and adolescent medicine and maternal and child health expert, from the Mom's Hierarchy of Needs site is one of the most enlightening health conversations I've had. She said, "My theory on menopause is that your body's like, 'oh, you're 50? Thank you for your service. I'm taking away your estrogen, now go die'. Although they took the word *replacement* out of *hormone replacement therapy*, it is actually a replacement. Your body took it away and we're putting it back to avoid the badness that can affect your brain, bones, and heart."

She has a unique perspective on big hormonal transitions— as both a pediatrician and maternal child health expert, she's studied and treated patients from their first periods through menopause.

Menopause Symptoms Can Be Hard to Discern

Until recently, treating menopause[12] was almost synonymous with treating its known symptoms, which vary, yet are generally considered "treatable" if they're hot flashes, painful sex, or frequent urinary tract infections (UTIs). But what's less known is that menopause also puts women at greater risk for serious illnesses. Sophia explained, "Replacing estrogen is not only to treat symptoms. We're seeing data that it can prevent osteoporosis.[13] And we've always known about its implications for cardiac health[14] and dementia."[15]

She recommended I read the book *Estrogen Matters* by Dr. Avrum Z. Bluming and Dr. Carol Tavris, which was fascinating. In it, they said,

> "Heart palpitations certainly get a woman's attention but many other symptoms that are also signs of menopause usually do not, symptoms such as severe dryness of the eyes and mouth, which many of which develop even when women are still getting regular periods. Or joint and muscle aches and pains. . . . . hot flashes, night sweats, difficulty sleeping, insomnia, difficulty concentrating, decreasing recent memory, decreasing energy reserve, bladder or urinary discomfort, more frequent UTIs, vaginal dryness, vaginal discharge or bleeding, loss of sexual desire, painful sexual intercourse, depression and sadness, tension and nervousness, mood swings, headaches, bloating, swelling of hands or feet, breast tenderness, aching joints, thinning hair, palpitations or racing heart, chest pains with exertion or weight gain around the abdomen."

Then went on to explain that if you experience any of these symptoms, you're generally sent to different doctors who specialize in each of these issues.

Vet Your Care Team

Although the first stop is often to see your OB-GYN, not every OB-GYN has the latest and greatest information about menopause. Sophia said, "There are approximately 1,300 menopause society certified practitioners[16] in the nation. I believe only about 20% of OB-GYN programs teach about menopause. And then there's the question of who's in charge of menopause, is it the OB-GYN or internal medicine? And your insurance may limit who's available to you.

Specialists are harder to get into and may be more expensive. But realize that doctors can't know everything." She recommends asking your doctors questions about their backgrounds and treatment plans. For example: "Have you had menopause training? How much have you had?"

According to the National Institute of Health,[17] "most women begin the menopausal transition between ages 45–55." If you're in the stage of life (i.e., 40 or older) when you could possibly be entering this transition, it's important to understand the main points and seek out a medical evaluation with a health care practitioner. All of the sleep, supplements, exercise, and healthy eating in the world will not undo the dramatic impact of declining estrogen and progesterone in your body. This often-underappreciated source of fuel and resilience is finally getting more attention in the women's health and innovation community. So, once you have your other sources of fuel in play—with movement, nutritional meals, sleep, and stress management, then you can better tap into your natural desire to learn and grow personally and professionally. That's what we're going to cover next.

Notes

1. https://www.heart.org/en/healthy-living/healthy-eating/eat-smart/nutrition-basics/mediterranean-diet
2. https://www.amazon.com/Sweet-Palate-Surviving-Rebuilding-Microbiome/dp/1538110474
3. https://food52.com/recipes/38532-beet-kvass
4. https://www.healthline.com/nutrition/food-toxins-that-are-concerning
5. https://ewg.org/
6. https://my.clevelandclinic.org/health/body/22353-estrogen
7. https://my.clevelandclinic.org/health/body/24562-progesterone

8. https://www.nia.nih.gov/health/menopause/hot-flashes-what-can-i-do
9. https://momshierarchyofneeds.com/2023/07/15/why-its-hard-to-stop-bouncing-from-one-sleep-challenge-to-another/
10. https://www.hopkinsmedicine.org/health/wellness-and-prevention/can-menopause-cause-depression
11. https://momshierarchyofneeds.com/2022/08/27/what-to-do-when-emotional-exhaustion-is-more-than-just-a-bad-day/
12. https://www.mayoclinic.org/diseases-conditions/menopause/symptoms-causes/syc-20353397#:~:text=Menopause%20is%20the%20time%20that,is%20a%20natural%20biological%20process
13. https://www.ncbi.nlm.nih.gov/pmc/articles/PMC5643776/
14. https://www.ncbi.nlm.nih.gov/pmc/articles/PMC10074318/
15. https://www.health.harvard.edu/womens-health/dementia-link-to-early-menopause
16. https://www.menopause.org/
17. https://www.nia.nih.gov/health/menopause/what-menopause#:~:text=Most%20women%20begin%20the%20menopausal,52%20in%20the%20United%20States

Chapter 12

Make the Space for Learning and Growth

"I'm here from Boston, too!" I smiled and asked, "What brought you to this conference?" We met standing in line for breakfast, during a conference in Brooklyn, New York. I put down my heavy laptop bag and plate, so that we could connect properly. I learned that she was also a writer and recently published a book. At the time, she had one child and her daughter was a couple of years younger than mine, who was four at the time, and my son was eight. She asked, "How do you make time to write? Or, for that matter, to get any work done at all with kids?" I laughed and said, "It's not exactly perfect, as you know. Traveling and even coming to this conference was hard but I've set up a lot of systems to streamline other things. Like meals, and I try to do one deep work block to write each week, usually I go to a coworking spot in my neighborhood or the library."

We continued to compare notes about childcare and exchanged business cards so that we could meet up in Boston. I said, "Sorry, I need to run for the next workshop. There's a session about setting up your website for search engine optimization (SEO) and I really want to learn about that."

A few minutes later, I was taking copious notes about the power of SEO and how to do it when publishing articles. Although I'll admit, before I started the research for Mom's Hierarchy of Needs, I was already a pretty solid writer. I was usually the person in the family who wrote time-sensitive or important letters, résumés, and helped edit proposals or papers. I also wrote heavily in my corporate jobs but marketing and other business writing was quite different than writing for an audience of moms. I also didn't realize when I started that having a website meant learning how to set it up and manage the mechanics of it. My husband is an engineer, and helped me a lot. If WordPress were giving out awards for the most customer support chat sessions, I am sure I would have won especially during the first two years. The technical aspects of managing a website are not my strength and never will be, but I've learned enough to ask the right questions and for many things now, hire the right people. My years of training to work in a corporate setting wasn't enough anymore; I needed a lot of new knowledge.

What Do You Want to Learn?

When I went to that BlogHer conference in New York, Mom's Hierarchy of Needs was still a passion project. There was no revenue or plan for it at that point, I just knew that moving to this type of writing and research was opening me up in a powerful way and I wanted to pursue the curiosity and feelings it was stirring up. As I shared in Section One, a lot broke for parents in the pandemic. Although some people have found new freedom to maintain healthier habits, where time previously spent commuting was replaced with a new routine enabled by hybrid or remote work, most people—especially most mothers—are still struggling to fit everything together. So, the idea of growing may feel completely impossible to you right now. But consider that there are many ways to learn new things and to grow, as a person, creatively, and in your career. With a little planning and strategy you can tailor a personal growth plan that works for your circumstances, responsibilities, lifestyle, and goals.

What Have You Given Up and What Have You Gained?

"Leslie, I'm really glad that you're here talking about this. It's been hard because both of my kids are under the age of five and my wife and I are trying to care for them while daycare is closed, but we both work full time from home now. There's just no time to do much of anything other than survive. I don't want to speak for the other parents here but I feel like since the pandemic started, there have been all of these amazing learning opportunities. Like virtual conferences and events and my childless peers are just soaking that up! I had planned to grow in my career this year, so I'm really worried I'm not going to be able to do that. How can I make time for growth?"

One of the early corporate presentations from spring 2021 was to a large group of people managers at a tech company. And during the question-and-answer session there was a dad with young kids who asked these questions about learning; several other parents since that presentation have asked a version of the same question. You may have a plan for your career. And whatever that plan looks like, you probably anticipated growth but didn't realize how mentally and physically stretched you would be with kids. Whether they are teething, learning to read, or learning to drive, they need you and your space for anything else becomes limited.

As the needs in your family change you may have inadvertently given something important up to make the space. For example, pre-kids, maybe you worked out every afternoon or listened to music in your car as you transitioned from the workday to home. Maybe you slept a certain number of hours consistently and then, when your child was potty training or otherwise sleep-regressing, suddenly your nights and rest become fragmented. It's easy for a pattern of sleepless nights and foggy days to become a decades-long adventure without some sort of intervention. Health habits are super important but what about the developmental side of self-care? You know, interests, fun, and learning are way up at the top of the Mom's Hierarchy of Needs framework. Okay, I feel you thinking "how can I possibly do that, Leslie? I'm still ruminating about how to get exercise in" but do not fret. It is doable; it just requires some new strategies and a gracious timeline. My learning and personal development have accelerated since having kids, largely because of having kids, so if it's of interest to you, we'll dig into making that happen in ways that suit your life.

Thought Starters

- Think about the rituals you had before you became a mom. Is anything missing?
- If you've been fortunate to gain new habits that make you feel healthier and happier, take note of what you've added. Also, if you have new additions, where have you made the space for these new routines?

Are You Ready to Get Creative?

There are countless studies that link play and expressing your creativity[1] to overall happiness, productivity, and growth. You might just be at a point where you want to get creative and learn something that doesn't necessarily translate to your career.

For example, adult coloring has become all the rage and a source of both creativity and stress relief for many people. Since the pandemic, moms in our study have shared they've taken up or rediscovered knitting, painting, playing guitar, sculpture, and writing.

There are countless ways that you can exercise your creative gifts. Don't feel the need to tie every moment of your day to work activities. I understand how compelling it is to do that because most of us are incredibly busy. But if a hobby, interest, or passion project leads to feeling more fulfilled, that creativity will likely spill over into improving other areas of your life.

By the Way, You Have Leadership Superpowers

"When you show up for parenthood, you're likely to unlock the capacity to collaborate more effectively, which is one of the critical skills that we need in the modern workplace. Almost all work is becoming team based," said Amy Henderson, author of *Tending, Parenthood and the Future of Work*.

There are critical leadership and career skills that parenting helps to unlock. During my first interview with Amy Henderson, I learned there's a field of research we don't hear that much about, called *work/life enrichment*, which relates to parenting. It's work/life conflict's happy twin.

Neuroscientists have validated what you've likely experienced: certain leadership skills can be very challenging to train people for, such as productivity, efficiency, collaboration, emotional intelligence, and even courage, which were enhanced for people who have hands-on caregiving responsibilities for their kids. This transformation applies to both birthing and non-birthing parents, especially in the first year. Keep in mind that these are desirable skills and what many innovative employers look for.

Okay, how would you like to augment your superpowers? So many choices! Don't hold back or try to offer up your "safety school" choices. What do you *really* want to learn? Mastering the art of negotiation? Public speaking with greater confidence or learning to speak a new language? You may be thinking about adding new skills to your repertoire that will enable you to grow as a person or take on projects that would be more meaningful in your work, community, or personal life. However, you may really want new functional skills, like glass blowing, basket weaving, or learning how to code.

Learning for Career Growth When You're Employed

For example:

- A promotion
- New functional or adjacent responsibilities
- Growing and leading a team
- Expanded network

There are lots of different ways to accelerate your career, if that is what you want right now, even if it stalled or shifted. What makes sense for you as a next step depends on your current professional role and what growth means to you. Growth might mean getting promoted and achieving the next level in your current functional role. If it's not a promotion to the next level but you want to take on new functional responsibilities, for example, if you are working in sales and want to become responsible for sales strategy or forecasting, you can use different strategies for that.

A first step might be asking some questions of your manager during the next one-on-one:

- **Ask about their assessment of your performance,** relative to what the organization expects for that next-level position. It doesn't have to be formal, but why wait for your next review? You might say, "I know we've been in survival mode as a short-staffed team but I'm eager to plan my career proactively. We had discussed possible promotional paths a while back. I'd love to get your thoughts on what opportunities may exist in the coming year."

- **Ask where there may be gaps that you can build a developmental plan around.** You might say, "I appreciate that feedback. I understand how important project management is to this team and I would love to be considered for the opening early next year. I've had project management experience in prior roles, but I'd love to learn more about how we do it here at XYZ organization. Whom would you suggest I talk with to learn more about the systems for our company?"

These conversations are rarely one and done, so after you get feedback on current strengths or gaps, proactively plan a follow-up on a monthly or quarterly basis to reconnect on progress. In addition to keeping your manager accountable, it demonstrates that you're willing (and comfortable) holding yourself accountable to this progress.

Making It Work

If you're not interested in a traditional promotion, such as reaching the next rung on the ladder for your organization, but want to take on fresh functional responsibilities, that's an option, too. For example, if you are working in marketing communications, but want to become more broadly involved in product marketing strategy, or if you're a benefits manager, perhaps you're interested in becoming a human resources (HR) generalist with non-benefits-related responsibilities.

These are just a couple of examples where your core strengths and functional expertise will likely need to be bolstered with some additional knowledge to make the kind of career shift you're interested in. And there's lots of different ways that you can do that:

- **Seek projects or assignments that would give you an opportunity to exercise new skills.** Your manager may be able to assist you with this, either by making introductions or providing you with the time or adding these learning experiences formally into your key performance indicators or goals.
- **Explore learning and development support through your employer.** Start with your HR team because some organizations invest in platforms like LinkedIn learning for their employees, or you may find that your employer will reimburse you to take certain courses. Some organizations create a separate learning and development budget that might include attending industry events or conferences.
- **Team up with a mentor or ally for ideas on how to grow your skill set in the desired area.** If you work for an employer, this could perhaps be someone in another department who can assist you in learning how to incorporate new skills for a different functional area into your current responsibilities. Again, it doesn't have to be a major move. It might just be that this person is going to help you get visibility to a project or even a committee within the organization where you can use those strengths. If you're self-employed or would rather not explore this with colleagues, consider an industry association or your mentors' and allies' recommendations for other ways to gain this new skill set.
- **Join your employer's affinity groups, such as employee (or business) resource groups (ERGs).** Again, back to the whole expanding your circle of support concept to find opportunities where you can potentially meet more people in the organization who will expose you to projects that

enable you to stretch yourself in different areas than your functional role does. Many larger organizations have ERGs for parents, caregivers, mothers, or women. It's where I'm often working for the employer side of my business, and those groups can be a wonderful source of work/life support, career guidance, friendship, and levity through your workdays.

- **Find industry associations or groups.** This doesn't have to be a formal group; you can even find LinkedIn groups for just about every professional role or industry you can imagine. There are also countless online groups, probably within your functional area or the place where you're seeking more experience. Meet people who are already doing that role, the one you really want to be in next. You may be surprised at how generous people are with their time, goodwill, and expertise.

- **Conduct informational interviews and gather input.** Again, this can be structured, such as setting up a series of intentional calls with people who have the expertise you're seeking, or less formal, such as attending a workshop or webinar to gather information about trends, needs, or responsibilities that might suit your expansion. You can even read (or listen to) a really great book about the topic you're interested in to kickstart your advancement. At the end of your exploration, you'll likely have more connections, clarity, and ideas about what you will need to put in place.

Many of us internalize society's messages about what leadership looks like. It typically doesn't look like a mom in traditional industries, but professional growth is for everyone. When you pursue your career aspirations, it can help you feel more fulfilled, financially stable, aligned with your values, and confident.

However, as we'll explore more broadly in this chapter, learning is learning. There does not have to be a professional connection. You might want to take up knitting or cross stitch, bowling, or pickleball, and if so, then please go after it!

Learning for Personal Growth or Professional Pivots

I've learned a lot about how I like to learn. What structures feel the most useful for you?

Think About Your Preferred Approach

Decide on your preferred learning modalities based on your personal style, the type of learning that's been effective for you in the past, and what your goals are for using this new skill or knowledge once you have it. For example, do you want to become a stronger negotiator, or do you want to make pottery? Sometimes you don't know what you don't know until you've tried it.

For example, although I'm very committed to running, I realized after running two Spartan[2] (obstacle course) races with a group of local mom friends that I wasn't very strong. At least, not as strong as I want to be—especially in my shoulders and arms—so I later sought a few personal training sessions at my gym and recommitted to strength training. I knew I needed to learn from someone how to lift heavier weights and safely incorporate it into my weekly routine.

Early in my business, I took several online courses that were asynchronous, such as watching a YouTube video about using Pinterest or listening to an audiobook about entrepreneurship. They were great for a deep dive on a topic in which I already had some familiarity or expertise, but for something that I wasn't as familiar with, they only provided a high-level understanding, and I found it difficult to implement that learning. For example, I read a great book about growing my social media following but when I needed to dig in deep and do something they recommended, it didn't really work. Although I have a lot of business experience, I don't have social media follower growth experience. When this happens, I realize I usually needed a live class, with an instructor or a direct one-on-one conversation with a consultant or coach. This is an insight into what stage of the learning process I was in that I didn't understand about myself when I first signed up for so many asynchronous or even synchronous group activities. Many of the group programs I went through were wonderful for me in the beginning. But once I wasn't a newbie and had more sophisticated questions to implement the learning, then it wasn't enough. There was one program on social media growth where I would sit through an hour and a half waiting for my turn to ask a question, which felt excruciating when I barely had time to eat during the rare childcare windows available to me. Once I really understood this about my learning style and needs, I stopped investing in those types of modalities when I needed to execute something I was unfamiliar with. Dance class is another great example. Although I danced for 20 years through my childhood and into college, dance is not something I like to learn online. I prefer being in person, physically in a class, and in a position where I can ask questions and see what the instructor is doing with her stance.

Find Your Time Slots

Now we're going to talk about the part that's often the hardest, and that's finding the time. I hope you have a few ideas about where you would like to start. Remember, where you start doesn't mean you are locked into a long commitment or direction. It's just a start. I'm going to explain a bit about my energetic space framework soon in this section, and then you will also have a more in-depth systems guide you can use for your implementation linked in the Afterword. You can use this framework to make time for just about anything, including learning.

Choose Experimentation

Please ease any worries about learning this new thing that you're interested in by giving yourself a short timeline to experiment with a new learning path.

- Are you starting from scratch? Or do you already have some of the skills and knowledge that you need for this? If it's the latter, what are your gaps?
- You might decide to focus on this learning path for 30 days or for 90 days or for the season (e.g., summer).
- Choose a time frame that enables you to feel a sense of ownership and provides enough time so you can take away something meaningful from the activity.
- Then, you can set a few time blocks that really work for your life and determine how quickly you check in with yourself on progress. And by "really works for your life" I mean it, so let me repeat that. Something that really works for your life! Please don't sign up for some sort of 5 a.m. thing when you're not a morning person, or a long commute or complicated set of certifications, unless that's exactly what you want.

Choose an Anchor Time of Day

I like to recommend that you start with morning routines because that may be the place where you have some freedom. Depending on the age and independence of your kids or your responsibilities at home or work there might be a window before you have to start getting ready for your day or your children's days but after you wake up when you can allocate space to this endeavor.

And remember, habits are really powerful (e.g., you want to do five minutes of a deep breathing exercise every morning after you wake up) because if you set a habit and you have a routine it's much easier to stay with it consistently. As I shared in Section One, our brains like habits because cognitively, they are less demanding than trying to reinvent your schedule every day or every week.

Late afternoons or evenings are another period to play with, which depends on your and your family's schedule and support systems. I know many more people work either hybrid or remotely now so that separation between a physical workspace and home may not be there. Some people have success making an emotional or symbolic transition, from work to personal, even if it's not leaving a physical workspace. Remember that brilliant tip from Dr. Caroline Danda I shared: to take a breath before transitioning from one activity to the next? She also would sit in her car before going into her home for a few moments after leaving her practice. For example, maybe you'd like to start learning how to paint and there's a class near your home before pickup for your kids, but you're often still keyed up with thoughts of the workday to-do list in the evenings. Perhaps commit to closing your laptop at a specific time on class days and go outside for a 15-minute walk to adjust. During that emotional transition window, you could listen to a podcast or a book about painting, seeing museums in Europe, or different styles of painting, or another new learning area that you want to develop for yourself. This helps you get excited about the class you've signed up for and use a transition to ease yourself into the nonwork mindset prior to starting your new routine.

Choose Your Modality or Format

There's an incredible amount of high-quality learning content in very accessible formats for which you don't have to sit down and commit to a class that lasts for an hour or two. If you can grab small bursts of time, especially if you're listening to something like a podcast or a book, perhaps this way of learning works for you. I started listening to podcasts and audiobooks while cooking dinner during the pandemic when I stopped commuting to an office.

If you are interested in learning something more intensive to complement your current expertise, and if it's something, for example, that you need to be accredited or certified for by an outside organization, consider taking paid time off if you work for an employer. You may not need to take an entire vacation day; some organizations allow you to take a half-day. Again, if you're in a traditional work setting your HR team or manager may be able to help offset costs or the time you need to allocate if the learning is directly related to your professional progression or well-being.

Let's say it's something completely for fun that requires a longer block of time, such as getting your scuba diving certificate or learning to sail. You might set aside a few days or an extended weekend to complete a course or workshop to develop this new skill. That might mean lining up, covering, or tying it in with a family vacation, or tacking on some days off when you have a work trip to a spot that is warm enough for you to scuba train outdoors, for example.

And if you put it on your calendar, even if it's six months from now, having it there can be a strong motivator to take the steps to do it between now and then.

Honor Your Learning Intentions

Questions to ask yourself:

- What do I want to take away from this new learning experience?
- What would feel meaningful to me?
- Do I have a time frame in mind for a particular goal, for example, getting certified in a new specialty like yoga or scuba or achieving a promotion to senior director by a certain time frame?

I know, I said you wouldn't have to do anything too aggressive, and you don't. Remember, you've already gained amazing skills as a parent. Just like Angela Duckworth says in her book *GRIT*, adopt a "growth mindset." You and your skills and knowledge are always evolving, but have some intention about what you would like to take away from this endeavor:

- It could be that you want to be certified in a new professional area, like becoming an executive coach.
- It could be that you want to be a belly dancer part-time, outside of your professional life.
- It could be that you're having a new baby and finally want to get that infant cardiopulmonary resuscitation designation.
- It could be that you just want to strengthen your negotiation skills before asking for that promotion or critical conversation skills to strengthen conversations with your partner at home, if partnered.
- If you've been tasked with pursuing additional education, then think about whether you need to have a formal accreditation or if there is an alternate course that is more accessible and friendly to your schedule in the near term.

So, take a moment to just think a little bit about what you want to accomplish. And **I** recommend having no more than two or three intentions for what you would like to achieve as learning goals in the near term.

Write Them Down and Be Specific!

For example:

- I want to strengthen my public speaking skills so I can give a TED Talk to my industry peers within the next year.
- I would like to learn to code so that I can begin to write my own software that makes my operational role more effective.

- I want to be able to speak French for when our family goes to Paris next year so I can order my meals like a local.
- I would like to get promoted sometime within the next year, so I am taking on new projects through our ERG that will give me experience with event planning or social media marketing.
- I want to knit a blanket for the new baby I'm expecting next year so she has something to pass down that I've made to her own children.

Those are just a few examples, but they are specific, clear, and if you keep those intentions in front of you, it will make the process and what you need to pursue next more available. If you gave yourself a time frame of 90 days to experiment, set aside 20–30 minutes on your calendar each month for a quick check-in with yourself.

Here are a few suggestions:

- How do I feel about this learning path so far?
- Does it fuel me or feel draining?
- Do I need to renegotiate—at work or at home—to get more flexibility or space to pursue this?
- Do I want (or need) to take time away from work or my environment to pursue this?
- Is it time to talk with my manager about how these goals fit with my career planning?
- What has been the best time slot to fit this in so far?
- What have I learned that I can implement in some way—whether for work, a passion project, creative endeavor, or my desire to unwind?

Remember, it's all about how you feel about this and where it fits within your priorities and goals. Be compassionate with yourself as you reintegrate learning into your routine. Celebrate the wins, even small ones, like carving out space to listen to an entire podcast or conducting your first networking call. I know you're thinking, "Leslie, come on, everybody says to celebrate wins"; well, that's because it works. We tend to be very self-critical and focused on outcomes only, a way of thinking that doesn't feel good when pursuing a long-term or ongoing goal.

Notes

1. https://www.fastcompany.com/90392816/the-relationship-between-play-and-productivity
2. https://www.spartan.com/

Chapter 13

Healthy Adult Relationships and Energetic Space

"Leslie, we need to change things up with how we do Christmas. I can see how stressed we both are. We're not excited like 'we get to do this,' we're treating it like 'oh, we have to do this,' and it's not enjoyable. And when we come to your house, we try to respect your space and when you stay here, it's like you guys take over. It doesn't feel like you respect our space." My sister and I were sitting alone in the car after dropping off my parents. I knew this was a conversation that we had danced around, in different ways for years, so there was a part of me that was grateful to have the opening. I also felt particularly exhausted at that point, with the stress of the past several months weighing on me so heavily that I wasn't sure how the conversation would go.

"I'm glad we're having this conversation because I don't like staying at your place. It's extremely stressful for me, too, maybe as stressful as it feels to you," I blurted out. That morning, she had asked me to clean up a blob of toothpaste my daughter had left in the bathroom sink upstairs. Something that felt particularly punishing at the time because in my own home, I would have let something like that go for days if not longer.

Now let me set the stage, my sister's home is pristine. Neat, organized, and well decorated because she takes a lot of pride in how her home looks and her family is very aligned about keeping the space tidy and functional. I always feel self-conscious when my not-so-neat husband leaves dishes in the sink, a soda can on the floor, or the kids mess up the shape of her couch cushions.

I remember what it was like to be neat, although in my heart I still think of myself that way. That was when I lived alone more than 20 years ago. "Fig [one of my sister's nicknames], I can feel the tension, but I already feel like I'm doing even more housework here than I do in my own home, and I pretty much do housework all of the time! It's the thing I hate to do the most and this is the one vacation we have most years. It's expensive and a big effort to come here so, I don't want to be stressed about every move. I cook a lot when I'm here and I'm doing grocery runs including Christmas dinner, which means a ton of shopping, dishwashing, and cleaning. The reality is I can't police my family in your home. It's hard enough to do in my own home, and frankly, as you know, my standards have dropped through the floor when it comes to how my home looks."

She nodded, she'd been to my place enough times to know that was for real. I also told her that by the end of the year, especially since becoming a full-time founder, that I was emotionally and physically spent. There was nothing left over for doing extra or even enjoying the holidays very much because of the massive lift involved. Many years I brought our unpaid bills I had ignored in the two months before our arrival and paid them gradually each night from her kitchen table. Most years, I still had holiday cards to send, gifts to buy, or client work to finish, and all I wanted to do was just sit outside in the sun and do nothing for a while. But, of course, that just didn't happen, not once.

"Why don't you train the kids, Les? They're not babies anymore; they should be able to help you and be much more involved." I winced because at the time, I was just really depleted. This was in December 2023, and I also felt that way in December 2022—both years were emotionally not great. So, at first her comment felt like more judgment than I already had for myself, but I also knew that she was right. Even though my head was splitting at the time, we ended up having a good initial conversation about it. That candid discussion opened the door for subsequent conversations, and back home, I prepped my family that we would likely stay at a hotel for most of our visits going forward or at the very least, for half of each visit. I also spoke with the kids about keeping up with their stuff, staying tidy, and reinvigorating the routines that have been slow to take hold, like their involvement with our household and dishes.

I'm very lucky to have the sister that I do because she reminds me of who I am, and I try to do the same for her. We speak to each other most days, in one form or another. How much time do you spend with your close friends and family, beyond the family members you live with? Motherhood is so beautiful and fulfilling you may forget that you've let important needs, including important relationships, go dormant. Although according to Pew Research[1] just over half of adults (53%) cite having one to four close friends, and after age 65, having five or more close friends; however, studies show that more people are lonely[2] than in previous generations. This was true even among parents who responded to our research study during the height of lockdown.

You may have heard about the book, *The Good Life: Lessons from the World's Longest Scientific Study of Happiness* by Robert Waldinger and Marc Schulz. I'll give you the five-second summary: happiness comes down to having quality relationships with friends and family. Of course, thinking about this challenge through the "mom lens," what shows up in the Mom's Hierarchy of Needs research, over and over and over again, is the high cost of emotional labor in our personal and professional relationships. Basically, this means not doing what we really want to do and doing what we think others expect of us instead or otherwise feeling the weight of not saying the thing we need to say.

Take a moment to inventory your adult relationships, outside of your partnership, if you are partnered. Can you tell the truth? Do you feel respected? Is there reciprocity? Are you taking time to reconnect with your wonderful friends and people who support you? Many of us do not make this time after we have kids. You may be lucky to have developed close friendships during drop-off, pickup, or at the playground. Many of my newer friendships have come from having children in the same school or neighborhood. However, don't just hover on the surface with the people you're close to. Friendship is about more than just companionship and polite conversation. It's having room to exercise emotional integrity.

Let's (Not) Play Pretend

The point here is that, yes, your friendships far and near are extremely important. However, as you think about which friendships and adult relationships you need to resume, pause, or grow, think about the connections where you can respectfully tell the truth and have a disagreement without it being relationship ending. That might be with a sibling—I have that with my sister and my cousins, too. There is a unique bond with family that differs from other friendships, and your sibling probably isn't going to try to tell you what you want to hear, at least not in my family, but privacy is also not a thing in Bajan families. We just don't do that. Which means up front

Healthy Adult Relationships and Energetic Space

you know that well-intentioned family members will be up in your business most of the time. Now, your family may run on completely different rules, and I realize not everybody is lucky enough to have siblings or a trusted relationship with their family of origin.

Do you have friends or other family who will tell you what you may not want to hear, but do so in a direct and loving way? Do you have the types of relationships where people will cheer you on, once you set your mind to something, even if it's not necessarily the path they envisioned for you? Are there people in your life who will champion your work, your decisions, and be a sounding board when you need objectivity? In Eve Rodsky's book *Unicorn Space* she describes "spiritual friends," people who will nurture and encourage your creative expression, which is another distinct lens to view your friendships through. Ultimately, what's important to you right now in this season might influence the friends you make the time and energy for.

Moms are expected to play "nice" at work and in life, even when the situation doesn't warrant it. We're encouraged to pull back during times when we have clear justification to charge forward, which often leads us to distrust our own instincts. Perhaps most important, we feel the weight of being judged for things we do or don't do, including what our children do or don't do. The emotional tax on moms is already quite high so why add to your burden with thin friendships? You know what I'm talking about: those connections that force you to behave in a way that isn't how you want or need to express yourself in that moment.

It's probably not surprising with the demands of child raising that friendships and healthy adult relationships may not be a top priority. Friendships, however, help buffer life's roller coaster ride, and people we love and trust can help us see clearly through obscure circumstances. This is the time; it's never too late or too early to build those connections that will sustain you through this season. If you already have close connections, where the trust and reciprocity is already in place, how can you make the time to nurture those relationships and build in the space for this important part of your well-being?

Although I am generally against multitasking over presence, there are natural ways to combine checking in with your friends without feeling like you've done yourself, your friend, or your task list a disservice. A voice call while walking, commuting, clearing, cleaning, or waiting in line tends to brighten our perspectives and help revive time we don't necessarily value into something a bit more joyful.

The height of the pandemic taught us that things we never imagined could happen on Zoom, like doctors' appointments, funerals, and elementary school. A live call, with or without video, doesn't have to take a lot of time. It doesn't have to be on a regular cadence, like I am with my sister, because even our daily check-ins go through unexpected pauses, when life gets busy or complicated. What's important is the candor and the reciprocity. Feeling seen and asking questions, seeking or receiving love and support whether you're ranting, raving, crying, or celebrating is a gift.

Commit to Making Energetic Space

Here. We. Go. This is a process you can use to tie together the themes you've learned throughout this book. As I've described, this concept brought it all together for me to exercise everything I've learned and shared with you. I call this *energetic space*. When I'm speaking with employee groups, which is a lot of the work I do for organizations, I often take people through this concept and allow them to practice with a scenario they're experiencing. Or I help them through a real-life scenario where they need support to create this space.

Energetic space has three parts to it (see Figure 13.1).

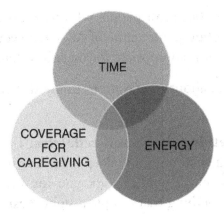

Figure 13.1 Energetic space.

It's that little intersection where the following can happen:

- **You actually have the time appropriate for the task you want to do.** So, for example, if you only have 10 minutes available and you want to take a walk, then it's fine to take a 10-minute walk. It can be incredibly satisfying but if you really want to unwind and watch a movie, and you only have 10 minutes, that's not going to work.
- **In addition to having enough time to do what you'd like to do, you have care coverage.** Especially when it's for self-care or deep work. Your kids are going to need to be in school or daycare, with your nanny, sitter, parents, or your partner (if you are partnered), or you'll need to arrange a childcare swap or playdate with your neighbor or trusted friends. If you're also caring for a special needs adult or senior, the coverage will look different, but you'll need care coverage in that scenario, too.
- **This time needs to be when you have the appropriate energy for the activity.** The example I like to give is training for a marathon. Many of us start our day early with our kids, so if you decide, you really want to train for a marathon, it's probably not going to work if your training begins at 10 p.m. You're exhausted by 10 p.m. Not

everyone is, but most people who have early starts to the day are. So, figure out a time of day where your energy and the time slot is appropriate for marathon training.

Then think about your options to use this energetic space to reset:

- **Do something that is self-reflective.** Try journaling or meditating or doing some deep breathing in a quiet space, where no one is going to ask you for anything, such as finding something that's in plain sight. Again, do it within an energetic space if possible.
- **Space to react.** Maybe you want to take that walk or call that friend or you really want to be in this PhD program and need to complete the application or write a grant proposal. Or this could be the time to find that specialist for one of your kids. You need the time, coverage, and mental and physical energy to tackle it.
- **Connection time is also really important.** As we discussed previously in this chapter, find those people, friends, or family who revive you. Or perhaps it's coworkers and people influential to your career who can help you network, if you're seeking new opportunities.
- **Navigate, physically.** Move from place to place to your events, travel, or to in-person activities. Give yourself the space to navigate with a buffer in between activities, including travel time and time to eat. How often do we forget to do that? It brings down the domino effect of having one thing go wrong and disrupt every other commitment you have that day.

There's a handy worksheet for you to access when you need it in the Afterword.

Next steps for your energetic space activity? Set a time block. Yes, that's right: take a look at your calendar but please do not get sucked into emails, instant messages, or social media alerts. Just find a block of time, because you know how easy it is to not do what you want if you can never get the time for it. You also probably know when you'd ideally like to do it, or what your "plan A" time is, so grab a block and create an appointment for yourself. Label it as a private appointment if you wish and it's a shared calendar or call it *me time* or *focused work block* and then set up a repeat. Mmmmm hmmmm . . . see, that wasn't so hard to do, was it? Make it weekly at first so you can look forward to it at the same time every week. My wish for you is once you have the system down, it's more fluid to manage the barriers and create back-up time slots.

Anticipate Barriers and Create Back-Up Times

There will be barriers, some anticipated and others not so much. Once you are comfortable making these adjustments, it becomes pretty fluid to adjust your daily routine within a few parameters or other time slots you can create. Here's an example that I often give when I'm speaking with parents or caregivers in the workplace on how to implement back-up slots based on the barriers you anticipate:

- **Set a small goal.** I want to walk every day for 15 minutes.
- **Allocate energetic space for it.** I will take a 15-minute walk after I drop off my kids at school.
- **Anticipate possible barriers.** After drop-off, other parents want to talk to me, or sometimes I have a meeting shortly after drop-off so I need to leave for work right away, and what happens when it rains?
- **Create a back-up plan (plan B, C, and possibly D).**
    Walking plan B. Response to another parent, "It's so good to see you! I'm now walking each day at this time; can we walk and talk together?"

Walking plan C. When the morning has another commitment, I'll do my walk during lunch time instead.

Walking plan D. If the weather is bad, I have my umbrella/waterproof shoes (or I will walk indoors at the local mall, or my office, or inside of the school, or on a treadmill at a local gym).

Enlist Support to Manage Barriers

Create a canned boundary response and paste it into your notes app or another place on your phone where you can reference it easily. For example, "I would love to catch up properly but I'm heading off to walk now" or "I would love to really talk with you, can we get together for a coffee on a Saturday at the park with the kids? I'm rushing to get ready for work now."

If you are partnered, "Hey, can you start taking care of drop-off so I can get more time for a morning walk?"

If you are not partnered or your partner isn't available, ask a neighbor, "Hi, I'm trying to get in some time for a walk in the mornings. Can my child walk with you and then I can pick up both kids and drop your children off in the afternoons?"

Remember to Keep Your Compass Focused on You

I'm an optimist and despite difficult experiences, some of which I've shared with you, I'm still "highly blessed" as we would say in the islands. I have been able to count on being happy or at the very least persistent and committed to a better path for most of my life. The emotional shifts after having kids really surprised me. I shared some of those moments with you because it's important to notice if your personality changes. I'm not talking about things you want to improve, such as becoming more patient or less sedentary. I'm talking about things that may be core to your signature style, such as being fierce, thoughtful, playful, or direct. If that starts to shift, know that you should pay attention because you are remarkable, you always have been, and you always will be. This book isn't about changing what's core, it's about enabling you to remember, reconnect with, and reveal it more often.

Although I have a lot more to do now than I have at any other point in my life, my conviction to do things that matter and align with my sense of purpose is stronger than ever.

Remember that BlogHer conference I mentioned in Chapter 12? Well, that next morning as I ran along the beautiful Hudson River, where I could see the Statue of Liberty and the glistening New York City skyline to my left, I saw a physical sign that stopped me. It was pretty beat-up looking, covered with grime from the cars passing by, and it might have had a dent or two, but it spoke to me so I photographed it anyway. It said, "Non-Stop Improvements," and it was posted by the New York City equivalent of public works. Basically, the sign wanted to let everyone know that all of the construction on the waterfront wasn't going to happen quickly, or end for that matter. They would continue to make infrastructure updates.

Learning is like that, too: it's nonstop. Before those early conferences, classes, and online workshops, all of my learning and development was paid for by my employers. I would go to amazing events only when they decided it was helpful. When I decided I owned my growth and that it was my responsibility, a gift I could give to myself, everything shifted.

In the past eight years since I started this movement, I've read hundreds of books (okay, I've listened to them on Audible or Libby—as I've shared, it's rare that I can sit down and read without interruption), interviewed hundreds of experts, and I've attended a lot of classes. Not the formal university classes many of us are used to, but informal classes at conferences, online, and during events. Being able to learn all the time is not only my favorite part of following an unplanned plot twist in my career, it's the part that keeps me charged and makes me feel alive. Like that sparkly, curious, confident childhood dot-connecting version of me.

Although I had become an expert in the work I was doing before, I'm grateful to keep learning, not just about what's relevant for my business but about everything that interests me. It's true, the cognitive demands of raising kids are significant, and as they grow, they increase. Potty training is hard, but helping children mature and develop their character and navigate friendships, academics, losses, or team environments also consumes a lot of mental calories. So, you'll face the dilemma of self-improvement in the way that you define it for yourself. You'll want the brain space you need to learn new things, while improving life for your family, and potentially your parents and friends, in parallel. But don't let the friction of that freak you out or push you away from your destiny. Because pursuing your interests, health needs, goals, and curiosities requires new information. It can be on your timeline and in ways that are right for you.

Remember, you've learned a lot already just by investing in the time to read this book. I started with free your mind in Section One, because until you know how much you're carrying emotionally and mentally or why you're carrying it, it's nearly impossible to make a plan that works. I had to learn a lot before I could begin to extricate myself from extra everything, including the expectations, cumbersome needs of others, and structures that didn't really serve me. Remember, once you have that clarity Section Two (ease your workload) is here for you to streamline. Return to it whenever you feel overwhelmed in the pursuit of your needs. What can you trim? Who can help you? Where can you find added bandwidth? What can you let go of? Cut with ruthless abandon to make the space for your health and everything in Section Three, which is the fuel for your future in the form of activities that nurture you and increase your energy for everything you are doing and want to do. Whatever they are—hobbies, exercise, date nights, girls nights outs, snuggle time with the kiddos, a relaxing meal, or mountain climbing—the point here is you get to make the call on the fuel sources. And of course, there are the preventative behaviors that experts have shared we need for our well-being, longevity, emotional, and hormonal health. Do the things you really love and want to do, along with critical needs for your body and mind like sleep and then boom! You become the most powerful, unstoppable, and fulfilled version of yourself. Living happy, fulfilled and fueled, is good for you, your family, and society.

That's why I wrote this: for you to live in that space of freedom to enjoy motherhood, in good health, along with everything else that defines you.

With love and gratitude,

Leslie

Notes

1. https://www.pewresearch.org/short-reads/2023/10/12/what-does-friendship-look-like-in-america/
2. https://pmc.ncbi.nlm.nih.gov/articles/PMC8948056/

Afterword: Tools You Can Use

Think of this chapter as a little bonus, something meaty to hold onto and revisit whenever you need to. Are you a systems thinker? Whether you answered yes or no I've created a few mom-friendly systems guides for you. I have to admit, I never thought of myself an operational person, but I am for certain things. There are areas where I can just go in and optimize, working backward from a goal and project manage to the finish line with such clarity that I am over-the-top effective. Other areas, well, not so much . . . I need the right amount of context, interest, and expertise to make something work better.

I have heard again and again from amazing moms like you (and dads, too, in my employer programs) how much they want to streamline things and especially the types of things that occur in our week-to-week lives. Like the daily dinner drill, being asked to volunteer our time, and carving out the space to do something (insert the blank here—run, read, or rest) when they have the "right" conditions. After a lot of reading, interviews with experts, insights from my research studies, and personal experiences, I could break down those conditions to make sure we approach these common needs with the energy not just the time required.

My gift to you for completing this journey is to share three systems thinking guides that until now have been available only to members of the Mom's Hierarchy of Needs community. I'm sharing some of our most prized ones here that you can use to reduce strain in your daily life and have some guardrails and ideas to get started and they're all available on www.momshierarchyofneeds.com/afterword.

- The ultimate guide to save time making dinner
- When to say yes to a volunteer assignment
- How to make energetic space worksheet

If you are seeking more helpful systems guides and a home to evolve these ideals and keep tuning into your needs, join us in the Mom's Hierarchy of Needs community! There's more information on our website, www.momshierarchyofneeds.com, and if you send a proof of purchase from this book to the form on the page https://momshierarchyofneeds.com/book, we have another awesome systems guide that we will send you with ideas on top of the Mom's Hierarchy of Needs activities that fit into anything from 15 minutes to a few hours of hopefully, energetic space. Yep . . . a little inspiration for when you're so tired that you don't know what you want to do for yourself with those rare extra moments. Plus a few other goodies . . . so please reach out, introduce yourself, and get the added resources.

Acknowledgments

There are many, many people who have been part of this journey, too many to list really. This includes every parent who has shared their voice, story, or input, in the Mom's Hierarchy of Needs research studies and the countless extraordinary experts I've interviewed for the website and for this book.

I'm grateful to my family, especially my children and my husband, Keith.

Also, to my sister, April, and her family, all of whom have provided encouragement, grace, support, and even creative business ideas when I really needed them.

I am also forever grateful to my late father, Douglas Forde, who would have loved to see this in print. He challenged me to become as resilient, spirited, determined, and creative as I am and inspired me to write, draw, dance, and believe "the best" is within my reach.

This book is dedicated to the world's best mother, mine, Marva Forde.

ACKNOWLEDGMENTS

About the Mom's Hierarchy of Needs pandemic research study.

This study began on March 21, 2020, and is still running. The results shared in this book are comprised of responses through March 20, 2024, with 3,411 parents participating, 97% of whom are women.

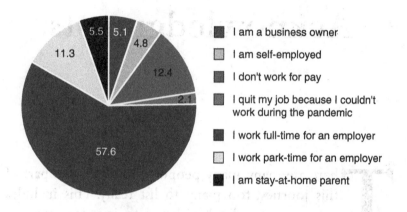

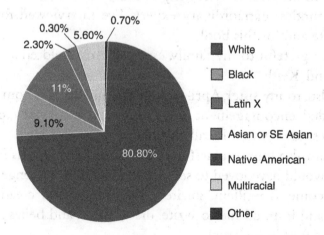

Acknowledgments

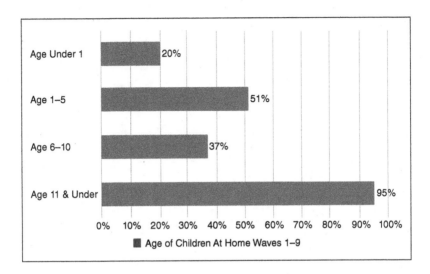

Index

A

academic support, for school-aged children, 115–116
activating micro-changes to environments, 170–171
adults
    caregivers for, 51
    self-care with support for, 112–114
affinity groups, 214–215
after-school youth/apprenticeship work programs (for teens), for childcare, 106–108
allies, 214
American Heart Association, 192–193
Amwell, 114
anchor time of day, choosing, 218–219
Anderson-Haynes, Sue-Ellen (nutritionist), 197–199
ApoB testing, 152
The Artists Way (Cameron), 52
athletics facilities, for childcare, 104–105
Atomic Habits (Clear), 182
Attia, Peter (author), 146, 155
Auger-Domínguez, Daisy (author), 85, 90

B

back-up care, 109–112
back-up times, creating, 233–234
barriers
    anticipating, 233–234
    enlisting support to manage, 234
batching tasks, 47–48
The Beauty of Success (Bracken-Ferguson), 135
black women, weathering and, 41
The Black Therapist's Guide to Private Practice and Entrepreneurship (Jackman), 159
blended families, managing calendars/expectations in, 173–174

BlogHer conference, 208, 235
Bluming, Avrum Z. (author),
    155, 204
boundaries
  about, 69–73
  asking for resources, 84
  delegating to cross-functional/
    direct teams, 85–86
  differences in leadership
    assignments, 88
  female leaders as allies, 82–84
  group power and, 90–92
  having canned responses for
    triggers, 92–94
  identifying what needs delegated
    or reassigned, 89–90
  managing people, 86–88
  personal power and, 81–82
  personal triggers and, 73–74
  psychological safety and,
    79–80, 90–92
  rules for, 80–81
  setting and maintaining, 74–79
  setting as a barrier to self-care, 10
  setting time limits for working
    under-resourced, 88–89
Bracken-Ferguson, Kendra
    (author), 135
brains, 34–36, 50
Brathwaite, Nichole C.
    (psychiatrist), 53
burnout, avoiding, 160

C

calendars, managing in blended
    families, 173–174
Cameron, Julie, 52
canned responses, having for
    boundary triggers, 92–94
capacity challenge, 10–13
care, back-up, 109–112
care team, 148–150, 204–205
careers, 23, 212–213

Careforce, 124
caregiving
  about, 7
  for adults, 51
  caregiver burnout, 12
  coverage for, in energetic
    space, 231–232
  ending careers for, 23
  stress and, 43
Carrot Fertility, 114
centenarian decathlon, 146
childcare support
  about, 95–97
  childcare collaborations
    for, 108–109
  for children of all ages and
    needs, 97–98
  failures of childcare, 101–104
  insufficiency as a barrier to
    self-care, 10
  lesser known employee
    benefits, 109–114
  mental complexity as a
    childcare cost, 100
  navigation help from
    pediatricians, 114–116
  strategies for primary coverage,
    98–99
  underused options, 104–109
children's activities, in Mom's
    Hierarchy of Needs, 6, 26
children's support, self-care
    with, 112–114
children's well-being, in Mom's
    Hierarchy of Needs, 6, 26
"A Christmas Carol" (Dickens), 33
church school, for childcare, 105–106
Clear, James (author), 182
cognitive (mental) load. *See* mental
    (cognitive) load
cognitive (over)load, reducing, 46
connection time, 232
context, boundary setting and, 78

country clubs, for childcare, 104–105
creativity, 210–211
cross-functional teams, delegating to, 85–86
Csíkszentmihályi, Mihály (author), 54
Curry, Michael (speaker), 41

D
daily movement practice, establishing, 181–183
Danda, Caroline (anxiety specialist), 24, 219
decision fatigue, 33–34, 37–41, 46
decluttering, 171–173
Deep Work (Newport), 70
deep work, staying in flow for, 54
Diamond, Rebekah (author), 114–115
Dickens, Charles (author), 33
digital health platforms, 112–114
direct teams, delegating to, 85–86
divorce, 126, 129–130
Drop the Ball (Dufu), 64, 123–124
dry weather, exercise in, 186
Duckworth, Angela (author), 221
Dufu, Tiffany (author), 64, 123–124

E
elders, 112–114, 154
emotional change, environmental changes and, 167–168
emotional health
  about, 157–158
  activating micro-changes to environments, 170–171
  avoiding burnout, 160
  barriers to good sleep, 162–164
  environment change and, 167–168
  environments and, 168–169
  identifying your stress tells, 159–160
  importance of rest for good sleep, 164–165
  importance of sleep for well-being, 160–162
  managing calendars and expectations in blended families, 173–174
  managing through scarcity thinking, 158–159
  overnights as a reset, 169–170
  reasons for sleep issues, 165–167
  reclaiming space within your home, 171–173
  solutions for sleep challenges, 167
  travel as a reset, 169–170
emotional support, getting after divorce, 131–132
employee benefits, childcare and, 109–114
employee resource groups (ERGs), 91–92, 214–215
employers, learning and development support through, 214
energetic space, committing to making, 230–233
energy inputs
  avoiding toxicity, 195–196
  hormonal health, 202–203
  importance of food, 192–194
  making one meal for everyone, 201
  menopause symptoms, 203–204
  partners and, 200–201
  planning meals, 194–195
  spicing up foods, 199–200
  streamlining meals, 189–192
  upgrading food favorites, 196–199
  vetting care team, 204–205
Environmental Working Group, 196
environments
  about, 168–169
  activating micro-changes to, 170–171
  boundary setting and, 78
  changes in, 167–168

Equal Credit Opportunity Act of 1974, 126
errands, tackling on foot, 178
estrogen, 202–203
Estrogen Matters (Bluming and Tavris), 155, 204
expectations, managing in blended families, 173–174
experimentation, choosing, 218
ex's, spouse sourcing with, 125–126

F
failures, of childcare, 101–104
Fair Play (Rodsky), 124
Fair Play method, 127–129
faith-based programs, for childcare, 105–106
family assistants, 135–137
family care, 102
family health history, updating, 154
fatherhood bonus, 5
fears, what are your, 23–24
female leaders, as allies, 82–84
fermented foods, 195
fertility support, self-care with, 112–114
financial support, getting after divorce, 130–131
Finding Flow (Csíkszentmihályi), 54
flexibility, with female leaders, 82–84
flow, staying in, 54
fluid intelligence, 31
focused work block, 233
food
  as an energy source, 192–194
  avoiding toxicity in, 195–196
  making one meal for everyone, 201
  partners and, 200–201
  spicing up, 199–200
  upgrading, 196–199
format, choosing for learning, 219–220
friends, for childcare, 108–109

From Burn Out to Lit Up (Auger-Domínguez), 85
Future of Wellness report (McKinsey), 7

G
gains and losses, 209–210
Geronimus, Arline (author), 41
Gomez-Carrion, Yvonne (doctor), 151
The Good Life (Waldinger and Schulz), 227–228
grandparent care, 102
Great Resignation, 37
green prebiotic powders, 195
Green Vibrance, 195
GRIT (Duckworth), 221
group power, using instead of personal power, 90–92
growth mindset, 221
gut health, 194–195
A Gut Feeling (Wise), 194–195

H
Harris, Shelby (psychologist), 164, 165–166, 167
Hartley, Catherine (professor), 171
Harvard Business Review, 23
health span
  about, 143–145
  health struggles as a barrier to self-care, 10
  organizing care team, 148–150
  personalizing approach to well-being, 147–148
  preventative testing, 152–153
  staying proactive with primary care/OB-GYN visits, 150–152
  systematizing preventative care, 153–155
  well-being and, 145–147
healthy relationships, in Mom's Hierarchy of Needs, 6, 26

Henderson, Amy (author), 211
Hendricks, Gay, 49, 64
Herring, Elaine Lin (author), 81
Hochschild, Arlie (sociologist), 71
Holmes-Rahe Life Stress Scale, 130
hormonal changes, as a reason for sleep issues, 165–167
hormonal health, 202–203
hormone replacement therapy, 203
hotels, for childcare, 104–105
household, in Mom's Hierarchy of Needs, 6, 26
household managers, 135–137
"How Moms Can Set Boundaries Without Feeling Guilty," 78
"How Same-Sex Couples Divide Chores and What It Reveals About Modern Parenting," 97
Hubbell, Kelly, 135–137
hyperfocus, 31

I

icy weather, exercise in, 187
industry associations/groups, 215
'informal breaks' fair play card, 130–131
'informal education' fair play card, 131
informational interviews, 215
intentions, 220–223
interests, in Mom's Hierarchy of Needs, 6
Irving, Shalon, 41
"Is Good Childcare the Answer to Better Mental Health?" article, 102

J

Jackman, Charmain (psychologist), 159
Jobs, Steve (CEO), 40
journaling, 51, 52

K

kavass, 194–195
ketogenic diets, 198–199
Kirke, Tara-Nicholle (CEO), 105, 172
Koh, Christine (entrepreneur), 24

L

lack of time, as a barrier to self-care, 10
leadership, 88, 211–212
learning
  about, 207–208
  for career growth, 212–213
  creativity, 210–211
  gains and losses, 209–210
  honoring your intentions, 220–221
  leadership superpowers, 211–212
  making it work, 213–216
  for personal growth, 216–220
  for professional pivots, 216–220
  what to learn, 208–209
  writing down your intentions, 221–223
logistical support, getting after divorce, 130–131
Lomas, Lucy (doctor), 151
Lorde, Audre, 18

M

Machung, Anne (author), 71
marginalization, 22–23
Maven Clinic, 114
McKinsey's Future of Wellness report, 7
me time, 233
meals, 189–192, 194–195
Mediterranean diet, 192–193
menopause, 202–205
mental complexity, as a childcare cost, 100
mental fog
  about, 45–46, 54–55
  creating flexible rules for repeated obligations, 46–48

mental fog (*continued*)
  importance of some structure, 53
  reducing cognitive (over)load, 46
  reducing decision fatigue, 46
  reducing overload using rituals, 50–53
  reducing routine outsourceable tasks, 48–49
  removing repeated points of friction/effort in professional life, 49–50
  staying in flow for deep work and self-care, 54
mental health, as a barrier to self-care, 10
mental (cognitive) load
  about, 33–37
  effect on decision fatigue, 39–41
  effect on influence of time scarcity, 39–41
mentors, 214
microbiome health, 194–195
Midi Health, 114
modality, choosing for learning, 219–220
Mom's Hierarchy of Needs, 6–7, 8–10, 26, 240, ix–x
"morning pages," 52
Motherhood Power Pause, 127–129
the motherhood penalty, 5–6
Motherly's *2024 State of Motherhood Report*, 7
movement
  about, 175–176
  choosing easy exercises over favorite exercises, 179–181
  doing errands on foot, 178
  establishing daily movement practice, 181–183
  planning walks, 176–178
  setting yourself up for success, 183–188
Mullainathan, Sendhil (author), 31, 61

multitasking, 230
Murty, Vivek (doctor), 11
My Sage Haus, 135
myth busting, xi

N

National Institute of Health, 205
neighbors, for childcare, 108–109
Newport, Cal (author), 70
night nanny, 161–162
norms, discussing with your partner, 121–123
notebook, next to bed, 51
nutrition
  avoiding toxicity, 195–196
  importance of food, 192–194
  making one meal for everyone, 201
  partners and, 200–201
  planning meals, 194–195
  spicing up foods, 199–200
  streamlining meals, 189–192
  upgrading food favorites, 196–199

O

obligations, creating flexible rules for repeated, 46–48
obstetrician-gynecologist (OB-GYN) visits, 150–154, 204–205
Outlive: The Science and Art of Longevity (Attia), 146, 155
outsourcing
  about, 119–121
  with an ex, 125–126
  clarifying what's expected of you, 123–124
  discussing norms and responsibilities with partners, 121–123
  easing your workload, 138–140
  family assistants, 135–137
  fighting for what you deserve, 129–130
  getting emotional support, 131–132

Index

getting financial and logistical support, 130–131
household managers, 135–137
inequity in divorce outcomes, 126
to paid support, 132–135
upleveling how you run your home, 124
written word, 127–129
overload, reducing using rituals, 50–53
overnights, for resets, 169–170
overworking, 43

P

paid support, outsourcing to, 132–135
Pandia Health, 203
Parent Like a Pediatrician (Diamond), 114–115
parenting
  about, 12
  parent stress, 60
  self-care with support, 112–114
partners, 102, 200–201
pediatricians, navigating caregiver support with, 114–116
Pennebaker, James, 52
people, managing, 86–88
perimenopause, 202–203
personal growth, learning for, 216–220
personal power, 81–82, 90–92
pods, for childcare, 108–109
post-nup document, 127–129
postpartum support, self-care with, 112–114
pregnancy bias, 23
pregnancy support, self-care with, 112–114
pre-menopause, 202–203
pretend, playing, 228–230
preventative health care, 43, 152–155

primary care visits, being proactive with, 150–152
priorities, revisiting highest, 63–64
proactivity, with primary care/ OB-GYN visits, 150–152
productivity tools, brain as, 50
professional life, 6, 26, 49–50, 216–220
psychological safety, 79–80, 90–92

R

reassignment, identifying tasks for, 89–90
relationships
  about, 225–228
  anticipating barriers, 233–234
  boundary setting and, 78
  committing to making energetic space, 230–233
  creating back-up times, 233–234
  enlisting support to manage barriers, 234
  keeping compass focused on you, 234–237
  playing pretend, 228–230
resorts, for childcare, 104–105
resources, asking for up front, 84
responses, for boundary triggers, 79
responsibilities, discussing with your partner, 121–123
rest, importance of for good sleep, 164–165
restarting, process of, 27–28
restorative activities, 17
rituals, reducing overload using, 50–53
Rodsky, Eve (author), 124, 126–131, 229
routine, as a positive, 53
routine outsourceable tasks, reducing, 48–49
rules, creating for repeated obligations, 46–48

S

Scarcity, Why Having Too Little Means So Much (Mullainathan and Shafir), 31, 61
scarcity thinking/mindset, 31, 61, 158–159
school, childcare and, 101–102
school-aged children, academic support for, 115–116
Schulz, Marc (author), 227–228
"second shift," 71
Seifert, April (psychologist), 36–37, 185
self-care
  barriers to, 10
  defined, 18
  in Mom's Hierarchy of Needs, 6, 26
  staying in flow for, 54
  using back-up care for, 111–112
self-reflective, 232
Shafir, Eidar (author), 31, 61
skills, exercising new, 214
slack, 62
sleep
  barriers to good, 162–164
  disruptions of, 17
  importance of rest for good, 164–165
  perimenopause and, 202–203
  reasons for issues with, 165–167
  solutions for issues with, 167
  well-being and, 160–162
snowy weather, exercise in, 187
solutions, for sleep issues, 167
SoulTour, 172
specificity, of intentions, 221–223
spicing up food, 199–200
spouse sourcing. *See* outsourcing
Sprocket CX, 36
state of mind, boundary setting and, 78
strategic trimming, 62–63
strategies, for primary childcare coverage, 98–99
stress
  caregiving and, 43
  in communities of color, 42–43
  identifying your tells, 159–160
  triggers for, 17
structure, as a positive, 53
support
  enlisting to manage barriers, 234
  insufficiency of, as a barrier to self-care, 10
swaps, for childcare, 108–109
symptoms, of menopause, 203–204
synagogues, for childcare, 105–106

T

Tavris, Carol (author), 155, 204
Teladoc, 114
Tending, Parenthood and the Future of Work (Henderson), 211
thought starters, 210
360° Girls & Women, LLC, 197
time
  choosing an anchor time of day, 218–219
  in energetic space, 231–232
  finding time slots, 217
  setting limits for working under-resourced, 88–89
time famine/poverty, 7, 45
time scarcity, 30–33, 39–41
TimeCheck® app, 182
tools, 239–240
toxicity, avoiding, 195–196
travel, for resets, 169–170
triggers, 73–74, 92–94
trimming, strategic, 62–63
2024 State of Motherhood Report (Motherly), 7
type 1 diabetes, 199

U

Unicorn Space (Rodsky), 124, 229
Unlearning Silence (Herring), 81

V

VO2 max, 147

W

Waldinger, Robert (author), 227–228
walks, planning, 176–178
weathering, 41–43
well-being
   health span and, 145–147
   improving your, 25–27
   obstacles to, 13
   personalizing your approach to, 147–148
   sleep and, 160–162
wellness app, 145
wet weather, exercise in, 186
"What Happens In Your Marriage When You Try to Set Boundaries," 78
Williams, Serena (professional athlete), 41
Wise, Heather (author), 194–195
The Women's Guide to Overcoming Insomnia (Harris), 164
work, boundary rules at, 80–81
working memory, 36–37, 50
work-life balance, 72, vii–viii
work/life enrichment, 211
workload, easing your, 138–140

Y

Yaktrax, 185
Yen, Sophia (doctor), 203
youth groups, for childcare, 105–106
YWCA/YMCA, 105

Z

zone of genius, 64